Sermons from the Days of Trump

Bob Melone, Jr.

&

Parson's Porch Books

www.parsonsporchbooks.com

Sermons from the Days of Trump
ISBN: Softcover 978-1-951472-40-5
Copyright © 2020 by Bob Melone, Jr.

Sermons from the Days of Trump

Contents

Introduction

Few things have influenced my preaching as much as the election of Donald Trump!

In 34 years of ministry, countless experiences have touched my heart and soul, and a variety of personal, church, national, and world events have influenced the way I have sought to interpret and apply Scripture to *my* life, as well as the way I have sought to help the people to whom I preach on Sunday mornings apply it to *their* lives. But nothing has had a more profound impact on what I share and how I share it than the behavior and administration of our nation's 45th president.

Like so many pastors, in seminary I was encouraged to preach with the Bible in one hand and the newspaper in the other. I have always believed that the Gospel is nothing if it is not political, and that there is no way to faithfully and effectively preach without dealing with politics of the day. But at the same time I have also sought to avoid partisanship, and to refrain from either demonizing one party or idolizing another.

But sadly, and tragically, on Tuesday, November 8, 2016, something happened that would dramatically alter the trajectory of our country, and influence my preaching for weeks, months, and years to come. At no point in my lifetime has an American President governed this nation with such blatant selfishness and narcissism, nor led the free world with such pompous arrogance and sanctimony. His lack of regard for those on the margins of our society, his naiveté with regard to the inherent racism of American life, and his disregard for the misogyny that plagues our world, can only be compared to history's most ill-equipped and uninformed national leaders. His moral bankruptcy and ethical infidelity fly in the face of all that is of God; and so if his presidency has NOT had an impact upon what is being preached in American pulpits, then something is tragically wrong with the American Church!

In my experience, Scriptural texts have never been as relevant as they have been for the past several years. The application of

Biblical principles to living life in 21st century America mandates that preachers embrace their prophetic voice. As was the case when the early Church sought to minister throughout the Roman Empire, faithfulness today will be defined by our willingness to speak truth to power, and by the courage we display in challenging the predominant theology of empire and the worship of national exceptionalism.

Scripture always has, and always will, set the agenda for my sermons. But when it comes to the application and interpretation of what I believe the Spirit to be saying to the Church today, for the past two years the various texts have set themselves in direct opposition to the policies and practices of the current administration. And sadly, in too many instances, these policies and practices have become the norm for the Republican Party.

The 'kin'dom, or reign, of God is about people loving mercy, seeking of justice, and walking humbly with the Spirit. The sermons included in this book are the fruit of my attempts to encourage the Church to do this. They are the result of the Spirit's movement in my life in the two and a half years following the election of Donald Trump, and I hope they continue to speak to you, the reader, today! Each sermon was modified only slightly to better fit this forum, with congregational examples removed to make the overall message more relevant to all readers. At times, they may appear to be overly punctuated, but they were written to be preached; and those punctuations guide my delivery. Further, since I often 'wander' from my printed manuscript I cannot fully guarantee that what I said when each sermon was preached, is exactly as it appears in this format. But it is close!

In several instances I have included an introduction to the sermon: a brief account about what was happening on the national stage in the weeks leading up to my message; the lyrics of a song or hymn used in worship the morning the message was given; some other element from worship on that particular Sunday; or a combination of the above. I have also included the Scripture texts for the day, and unless otherwise noted they are from the New Revised Standard Version.

My hope and prayer is that all of these messages will inform both your faith AND your politics; for as our walks with God are deepened, so too should our walks with one another. At times our faith is indeed intensely personal, but it is never private. It is lived out in our world, and thus our civic life cannot help but be impacted by the faith we profess with our lips.

If these messages offend you, be sure that it is ME doing the offending and not Scripture or the Spirit. For if it is either of them, that is between you and God. But if it is indeed me, I apologize. My goal is never to offend, only to be faithful.

Part 1: Year 1

Evangelism for the 21st Century:
Simple Acts of Service
November 13, 2016
(The Sunday after the election)

We worship you God of our fathers and mothers;
Through trials and tempest our guide you have been.
When perils o'er take us you will not forsake us,
And with your help O Lord our struggles we win.
("We praise you, O God", verse 2)

Acts 2:43-47

Awe came upon everyone, because many wonders and signs were being done by the apostles. All who believed were together and had all things in common; they would sell their possessions and goods and distribute the proceeds to all, as any had need. Day by day, as they spent much time together in the temple, they broke bread at home and ate their food with glad and generous hearts, praising God and having the goodwill of all the people. And day by day the Lord added to their number those who were being saved.

Acts 4:32-37

Now the whole group of those who believed were of one heart and soul, and no one claimed private ownership of any possessions, but everything they owned was held in common. With great power the apostles gave their testimony to the resurrection of the Lord Jesus, and great grace was upon them all. There was not a needy person among them, for as many as owned lands or houses sold them and brought the proceeds of what was sold. They laid it at the apostles' feet, and it was distributed to each as any had need. There was a Levite, a native of Cyprus, Joseph, to whom the apostles gave the name Barnabas (which means "son of encouragement"). He sold a field that belonged to him, then brought the money, and laid it at the apostles' feet.

I completely freaked the girl out!

It was a Saturday morning back in September, a week after I had preached on the story of Jael, from the book of Judges, and I was at the Old Town Farmers Market in Alexandria, VA. Now if by chance you don't know the story of Jael – J A E L – this is it in a nutshell. When the Israelites were doing battle with the Canaanites, a woman by the name of Jael invited Sisera, the commander of the Canaanite army, into her tent under the guise of trying to help him. He thought that she was attempting to save him from the Israelites; but once he was hidden under a rug, she drove a tent peg into his temple and killed him. That's the story: no doubt one of the oddest and most violent in all of Scripture!

It's also a story that is unfamiliar to most people; and so when I saw a new vendor at the market with a large sign that said, "Jael's Bagels," well I got kinda' excited. I had never seen that name Jael anywhere but in the book of Judges; and as a pastor, those kinds of things excite me!

Needless to say I make a b-line to the tent, suddenly craving a good bagel; and I asked the young woman who was behind the table if she was Jael. "Oh no," she says, "I'm just an employee."

"Well do you know the story of Jael in the Bible?" I asked . . . way too enthusiastically.

"Nnnnno," she said, hesitantly, and with raised eyebrows.

"Well I'm a pastor," I said, "and I just preached on the passage last week!" She continued to look at me, confused, and said nothing.

"She was a woman who killed the leader of an army that was fighting God's people by driving a tent spike into his temple! Can you believe that?"

"No," she again said, hesitantly, with God only knows what kind of thoughts rolling around in her head.

The little girl in line behind me was looking at me like I was absolutely crazy, and it was only then, that I realized I was probably being a little overbearing! I immediately began thinking about this sermon series, "Evangelism in the 21st Century," and thought this was probably NOT the best way to be an evangelist! But I love talking about God, and Scripture. It energizes me! Breaking stereotypes about Christians and challenging long held but ridiculous ideas and beliefs: that all animates me. It's why I love the church as much as I do. And it's why I believe that in spite of our flaws, the Church is this world's only hope.

Now I don't believe this to be true of the crazy side of the church – the rigid, paranoid, dogmatic, condemning, fire and brimstone church. But I do believe it to be true of the sane side: the portion that knows what it means to seek justice, love mercy, and walk humbly with God. That is the part of the Church that inspires and motivates me; and it's the part of the Church that I think pastor and poet Barrie Shepherd was writing about when penned the poem, "Why still go?" – which appeared in the August 2016 issue of "The Christian Century."

> For all their quirks and quibbles, all their foibles,
> squabbles, even downright donnybrooks,
> I find my people there.
> Recalcitrant, to be sure, concerning this issue,
> or that. As reluctant as those first followers
> to accept what fairest Jesus brought to life.
> Yet singing the same sweet songs.
> Murmuring familiar prayers.
>
> For all my weary, reasoned doubt,
> the continuing disillusion and despair
> of this already blood-drenched century,
> for all my anger at her blind echoing
> of the worst that hides in all of us . . .
>
> come Sunday morning, somehow,
> I still find myself in church.

Beautiful, isn't it?!

You see, in spite of the many errors of our past, I still believe with all my heart and mind and soul that we, the people of God, are the world's greatest hope! We don't just GO to church. We ARE the church! WE are the risen body of Christ in the world today, and while far from perfect, God is still at work in us, thru, and yes, often in spite of us! WE are the ones empowered to tell people about the amazing love of God. WE are the ones equipped to care for those in need: selling our possessions and growing generous hearts. WE are the ones who know that everything we have is to be shared, and that the common good should always be our common goal. We know that all we have is for everyone: stranger and alien, immigrant and refugee, Black and Brown, Gay and Trans, rich and poor. None of that matters to God. And as the people of God, we're called to share everything! That is the point of both of this morning's readings from the Book of Acts, ones normally read only on Pentecost Sunday.

Last Monday I attended a continuing education seminary held up in Burtonsville MD, and author and pastor Brian McLaren spoke on his new book, "The Great Spiritual Migration." Now I've spoken about Brian before, but if you've still not yet read any of his works, then this book is a must. It's my reading material for this Thanksgiving week at the beach, and I can't wait to dig into it. And what has me so excited is that Brian once again nails many of the problems facing the Church today. We've talked about many of them here; but the one most relevant for us this morning, as wrap up this series on sharing our faith has to do with what Brian claims to be the Church's migration away *from* belief, and *toward* behavior.

Brian's contention is that for hundreds of years now the church has very simply not been in accord with the heart of the early community of Christ-followers. For them, faith was regarded as a way of living: which is why Christians were called "People of the Way." But today, we have allowed our faith to become little more than a way of believing. And that is simply not what Jesus' life was all about. If that is what evangelism has become, inviting people to little more than a way of believing, then why are we surprised that people want nothing to do with Church?

This is one of the most important migrations taking place in the emerging church today; and it is forefront in the hearts and minds of many of us who have had to walk away from the evangelicalism of our youth. We have finally discovered the importance of migrating from a mere system of beliefs, to a loving way of life! And this is the type of community we see being described in this morning's Scripture readings from the Book of Acts. It's what we know to have been at the heart of Jesus' ministry in the world, and thus it is the ministry to which the Church is being called today.

That is why the final S in my ROSES acronym describing evangelism for the 21st century is 'Simple acts of Service.' A fifth way to share our faith is by showing kindness to, and loving, those whom God has put in our lives! When you think about your witness to the people in your life, this is what we need to be thinking about. We don't need to be worrying about what they 'believe' about heaven or hell. We don't need to try and convince them to 'believe' in things like the virgin birth or the bodily resurrection. Sharing our faith with them is NOT about getting them to 'believe' in the doctrine of the Trinity or Substitutionary Atonement. Instead, how about we just learn to serve them, and to love them, right where they are?

This is what "Simple Acts of Service" is all about. It's about just learning to better love others. It's about Jesus' call to be kind, and compassionate, and caring! After all, THIS is how people will know that we are Christ's disciples: by our love for one another! It's what the youth group gave testimony to yesterday when they worked down at the Central Union Mission. That kind of service is evangelism; and it's the kind of witness that the world so desperately needs today!

Five hundred years ago, the Father of Presbyterianism, John Calvin, sought to make all kinds of much needed correction to the Church of Jesus Christ . . . to reign in some of our wanderings . . . and to straighten out some of our thinking that was leading people astray! And in so doing "Tulip Calvinism" was born. But TULIP Calvinism is about doctrine. It's about right thinking, and right belief. TULIP stands for things that Calvin thought Presbyterians were supposed to BELIEVE: Total Depravity, Unconditional Election, Limited Atonement, Irresistible Grace, and 'Perseverance of the Saints.' These are the so-called 'right beliefs' that were at the heart of Calvin's teaching.

But friends, faith, or that to which we give our hearts, is so much more than mere belief. It is so much more than mental ascent to certain set of doctrines, truths, or creedal statements. Jesus was, and remains, far more concerned with our behavior . . . LOVING behavior; because Jesus knew that beliefs don't change the world. But behavior does!

Right belief can never become our goal. Jesus reminds us again and again that God is concerned about our how we live, and about our understanding of community! And what does that community look like? Well, certainly, it involves the way we speak about and treat women. Surely it involves the way we welcome and care for the Muslim immigrant, or the way we defend and provide for the refugee. It has to have something to do with the way we stand beside Brown and Black brothers and sisters, struggling in a system that is rigged against them!

When Jesus tells us to pray that God's will might be done on earth as it is in heaven; notice what he is saying. First off, he's telling us that faith is NOT about believing in some kind of escape plan, wherein we focus on leaving earth so that we might make it to some kind of heaven in the afterlife. Second, he's telling us that the 'kin'dom of God is meant for this world, here and now, and that it actually has very little to do with an afterlife. And third, he's making our mission in this life very clear – and it's nothing more and nothing less than making God's 'kin'dom a reality. It's called realized eschatology – wherein Jesus message is seen as above all else, a way of life, in which we love others thru simple acts of service, so that the reign of God might become a reality in our world.

That, Church, is evangelism! And think about it. What if this is what the Christian Church was known for: above all else, lovingly and serving others? I know we've established hospitals around the world, and all kinds of schools and care facilities for those with special needs, and the aging. But that is becoming more and more rare these days . . . which is likely why when most people think of the Church today, this is NOT what comes to mind. Today, when most people think of the church, they think of out-of-touch communities, where everyone is angry at changing sexual mores and thinks that climate change is a conspiracy theory! That's what the world thinks about us today. We're anti-gay and anti-science hypocrites! Look it up. Google it! This is what people think about us today.

And sadly, because so many in the White, evangelical Church are responsible for the election of Donald Trump, such attitudes are only going to be magnified over the next few years. So before I close this morning, let me say a few things about what happened last week.

Some of you are here still rejoicing over the outcome of Tuesday's election; and some of you are here with a grief that feels overwhelming. And such conflicting emotions are not uncommon following national elections. But this year the conflict is especially poignant; because this year the issues facing us go way beyond partisan policy issues. Perhaps unlike any other election in our lifetime, many of the issues raised in this campaign cycle have to do with character issues. And friends, the Body of Christ ALWAYS has a responsibility to speak to character issues. Both of our candidates forced us to talk about honesty and integrity, ethics and morality, decency and respect; and while such traits should be important to all people, they are particularly important to those of us who claim to be followers of Jesus.

So regardless of where you stand this morning, regardless of the thoughts and emotions that you have brought to this time we have together, regardless of your political party or who you voted for, we need to remember, especially now, that we are always citizens of **God's** 'kin'dom, before we are citizens of the world's kingdoms, even a kingdom as great as America. And we need to behave, and act, and vote, and live as such. As citizens of God's 'kin'dom, our goal must always be Christ-likeness. And nothing can or should ever be put before that goal.

In two months, Donald Trump will become the 45th President of these United States of America. And as followers of Jesus who also happen to be citizens of the United States of America, we have a responsibility to work with him in the accomplishment of all that is right and good and kind and faithful – a responsibility that we all have all the time, and after every national election. But we also have a responsibility to stand up and resist anything and everything that might seek to push against the things of God. We must never betray the Gospel in an attempt to further a political agenda; for we have another agenda – and it is not the agenda of either political party. It is the agenda of God.

So, when our elected officials work to uphold those values that are central to our faith, values that lift up the dignity of ALL people, as Jesus did; regardless of race, religion, gender, class, citizenship, ableness, or sexual orientation; then we, as people of faith, need to gladly comes alongside of and work with them to be about the work of governing this nation. And, similarly, when our elected officials fall short of these great aims, you better believe that we need to be the ones to speak up and advocate for those on the margins! For we are the people of God, the church of Jesus Christ: and our agenda is radically different from the kingdoms of this world.

Finally, because the Church always speaks with extra grace to those hurting, let me simply say to you who have been weeping for the past five days. God is god regardless of who is in the White House. Our faith is not built upon the Democratic Party, the Republican Party, or even a government. Ours is a faith built upon the rock that is Christ's love, justice, and yes . . . simple acts of service.

On my way into the office this morning I heard someone being interviewed on NPR, and I'm sorry I don't know the name of the program or the person who was speaking, but she was clearly a person of faith. And she was talking about darkness. Her point was that the resurrection took place in a tomb, a cave, with a boulder over the opening that shut out any and all light. THAT'S where the resurrection occurred: in the darkness! Not a single ray or beam of light saw it happen, because it took place, in the darkness.

Church, I found hope in that reminder this morning; for perhaps indeed, resurrection can only come, in the darkness.

As followers of the Risen Christ, that is our witness . . . that even in the deepest darkness, resurrection comes. So may that be our encouragement this morning. And may it prompt us to always strive to be God's people in the world, walking according to the way of Jesus, and thru simple acts of service, transforming out little corner of the planet.

That is our charge. That is our goal. Even, and perhaps especially, when darkness appears to reign.

Amen? Amen!

Christmas Classics –
Rudolph the Red-Nosed Reindeer
December 11, 2016

Christ, eternal Sun of justice, Christ, the rose of wisdom's seed,
Come to bless with fire and fragrance
hours of yearning hurt and need.
In the lonely, in the stranger, in the outcast hid from view:
Child who comes to grace the manger
teach our hearts to welcome you.
(Now the heavens start to whisper, vs. 3)

Isaiah 11:1-9

A shoot shall come out from the stump of Jesse, and a branch shall grow out of his roots. The spirit of the LORD shall rest on him, the spirit of wisdom and understanding, the spirit of counsel and might, the spirit of knowledge and the fear of the LORD. His delight shall be in the fear of the LORD. He shall not judge by what his eyes see, or decide by what his ears hear; but with righteousness he shall judge the poor, and decide with equity for the meek of the earth; he shall strike the earth with the rod of his mouth, and with the breath of his lips he shall kill the wicked. Righteousness shall be the belt around his waist, and faithfulness the belt around his loins.

The wolf shall live with the lamb, the leopard shall lie down with the kid, the calf and the lion and the fatling together, and a little child shall lead them. The cow and the bear shall graze, their young shall lie down together; and the lion shall eat straw like the ox. The nursing child shall play over the hole of the asp, and the weaned child shall put its hand on the adder's den. They will not hurt or destroy on all my holy mountain; for the earth will be full of the knowledge of the LORD as the waters cover the sea.

Isaiah 9:2-7

The people who walked in darkness have seen a great light; those who lived in a land of deep darkness — on them light has shined. You have multiplied the nation, you have increased its joy; they rejoice before you as with joy at the harvest, as people exult when dividing plunder. For the yoke of their burden, and the bar across their shoulders, the rod of their oppressor, you have broken as on the day of Midian. For all the boots of the tramping warriors and all the garments rolled in blood shall be burned as fuel for the fire. For a child has been born for us, a son given to us; authority rests upon his shoulders; and he is named Wonderful Counselor, Mighty God, Everlasting Father, Prince of Peace. His authority shall grow continually, and there shall be endless peace for the throne of David and his kingdom. He will establish and uphold it with justice and with righteousness from this time onward and forevermore. The zeal of the Lord of hosts will do this.

It's the proleptic nature of the Gospel! Who remembers what that is?

Good!

The proleptic nature of the Gospel is the 'now and the not yet' of God's kindom here on earth – the recognition that while Jesus does in fact offer us a new way of living, the complete fulfillment of God's desires for creation have not yet been realized. The peaceable kingdom that Isaiah writes about, where the wolf lies down with the lamb, and the earth is full of the knowledge of God – they are both experiences that we can all live into here and now; but at the same time they wait for us in a future that is yet unknown. 2000 years ago, in the "root of Jesse", Jesus, humanity realized that Light had indeed come into the darkness. But the endless peace and justice that we pray for each Sunday, that time when 'God's will is done here on earth, as it is in heaven,' well . . . that is still something that creation has not experienced in its entirety!

This is the proleptic nature of the Gospel – the 'now and the not yet' of Advent – when we celebrate what WAS, and IS . . . in Jesus, but when we also anticipate what WILL BE. And this should shape our understanding of the gifts of this season in which we find ourselves. Week one of Advent we considered God's unconditional love for creation; and last week we looked at the hope that comes with the realization that each of our lives is important to God. Now this morning, we turn to the candle of peace: a peace that is born in nothing less that than the justice of God. And like love and hope, peace is something each of us can know today, even if in just a small way. But because of the justice that gives birth to it, it is also something that the world does not yet know completely. Justice is something we must all be pursuing all the time; for the world can never know peace, until it knows justice! The two go hand in hand, and without justice, peace will remain elusive.

Now there are glimpses of peace and justice all around us, especially this time of year. And those glimpses should motivate and inspire each of us.

One cold December day in New York city, a 10-year old little boy was standing in front of a shoe store, peering into the window, barefoot, and shivering. It didn't take long for an elderly, well-dressed woman to approach the little boy and say, "Young man, you look like you're freezing!"

The little boy said, "I am. That's why I'm asking God for a pair of shoes!"

The lady took the little boy by the hand and went into the store. She asked the clerk to get some socks, and then inquired whether or not they had a basin and towel. The salesclerk quickly brought out a basin of warm water and an old towel from the storeroom, and the lady took everything to the rear of the store. Removing her gloves, she knelt down, and gently washed the boy's cold little feet. After drying them with the towel, she put on the pair of warm wool socks, and then had the salesclerk fit the little boy with a brand-new pair of shoes.

Before leaving, she tied up a few extra pairs of socks in a small bag, and then said to the boy, "I hope you will be a little warmer now!"

As she turned to go, the grateful little guy caught the woman by the hand, and looking into her face, with tears in his eyes, he said "Are you God's wife?"

Church, this kind of mercy is always on display in the peaceable kingdom that Isaiah is speaking about in this morning's Scripture passage. And the justice that should follow it, the justice that comes when we move beyond just caring for cold and homeless little boys, and that also seeks to take that next step to address and alter the systems and structures that allow for such conditions to exist; when THIS becomes the reality of our world, then peace can and will reign.

You see, peace is so much more than just the absence of war. In the Hebrew world, the concept of peace, or shalom, is wholeness, and rightness: where things are exactly as they are supposed to be! This is the peaceable kingdom about which Isaiah writes. And that is why peace can never be found without justice; and why some of the greatest peacemakers the world has ever know are people who have sought to make wholeness and rightness, the well-being of all creation, their life's goal! They are the world's greatest peacemakers; for they were justice-seekers as well!

Now interestingly, and perhaps only because of this sermon series, I recently noticed how many of our classic Christmas movies and television specials have been devoted to matters related to justice! Justice is at the heart of Dickens' "A Christmas Carol", and justice is hinted at in both "How the Grinch Stole Christmas" and "It's a Wonderful life." This whole idea of the holidays being about much more than selfish acquisition, but rather caring for others, is at the heart of so many of these Christmas stories. And it is even found in this week's "Christmas Classic": one that first aired on TV in 1964 – Rudolph the Red-Nosed Reindeer.

Sam the snowman, whose recognizable voice is that of Burl Ives, tells the story of Rudolph, who, after being ousted from reindeer games because of his red nose; teams up with Hermy, an elf who wants to be a dentist, and Yukon Cornelius, a prospector looking for silver and gold. Together they set out to search for a place to call home, and along the way, in the midst of a variety of encounters with the Abominable Snow monster, the three outcasts stumble upon a very special island knowns as the "Island of Misfit Toys!"

It's a great scene: where 'Charlie in the Box' and all the other toy 'misfits', are shown love, the first gift of Advent, and then given hope, the second gift. But in the end, peace comes only when they experience a form of justice, that gives them a home, on Christmas morning, in the caring arms of an eager little girl or boy!

Friends, Advent and Christmas, faithful and Christ-like living, they are all about seeking the peace that can only come about when all the people of the world, particularly those on the margins, experience the justice of God. And this must remain at the forefront of our holiday celebrations.

In today's Family Sunday School Class, we packed more than 30 bags of food that will be distributed by New Hope Housing this coming week, to families living on the margins of our society right here in Mt. Vernon. That's Advent. That's Christmas! And perhaps today, more than ever, we need to keep such work, and service, and mission, in the forefront of our minds. Because too often such behavior is NOT the norm. Even we in the church struggle to make this our priority.

We who claim to be followers of Jesus must be 'pro-lifers' in the truest sense of the word – not just anti-abortion, but truly pro-life, in that we care for the poor, and the homeless; the widow, and the orphan; the single father and mother; the alien and the immigrant looking for honest work. That is what it means to be pro-life – to be an advocate for any and everything that welcomes as many people as possible into the health and wholeness of God, into that peace that the Bible says, "passes all understanding!"

This is the third gift of Advent. Peace! Peace that moves beyond the mere absence of war, and that rather seeks the justice it is at the heart of shalom; justice that includes things like living wages, health care, gender equality; that rejects mass incarceration, religious oppression, and a color blindness that does little more than mask our color bias. That is justice; and it's the kind of justice that Christ-followers need to be seeking during Advent, and Christmas, and throughout the year. It is a justice that seeks to ensure that all people will have a roof over their heads, food on their tables, and perhaps most importantly, equal opportunities and access to providing these basic necessities of life for themselves. In order for the Advent gift of peace to be received by anyone, friends, these are the things we need to be about. This is the peace-bearing justice that is promised by the prophets; and it's the song that each of us needs to singing, even when it appears as though that is NOT the song the world wants to hear . . . even when we feel as though it is a song that alienates, and exiles us from others.

Last week, Wilson Gunn, National Capital Presbytery's General Presbyter, wrote in his December newsletter article about Advent being a season of exile and displacement. "It's a season" he says, when we remember "a young, unmarried teenager who walks toward her considerably older, cousin's home in the hills, where she will hide the embarrassment of her pregnancy and avoid the probable violence toward her person from those in the village of her birth – violence feared from neighbors she has known all her short life." As we remember that lonely journey, that sense of her being exiled and displaced, some of us can relate, can't we?

Can you? Can you relate to those feelings? Wilson was talking about Church leadership in this article, and he quoted George Kingsley, who says that leadership is learning "the song of the tribe, in order to SING the song of that tribe, so that others can find THEIR place in the song, AND so that then together, we can ALL write the next verse."

Well, I don't know about you, but lately, I've been having trouble hearing the song of my tribe. Like Mary, exile, and displacement, even loneliness – they have been at times too real for me. I know they have been too real for too many of us! Other songs have replaced the song of the misfit – and all we seem to be hearing these days are songs of power and domination, songs of hatred and anger, songs of fear and frustration.

But do not despair Church; for the song of our tribe IS STILL being sung, and in more places than we realize. And I am confident that in the coming months and years, it is a song that our nation and our world is going to hear with renewed vigor: songs calling all of us to a ministry to the misfits, to those on the margins; songs reminding us that in fact we are all misfits, and that we are all in need of the peace the only God.

So listen for the songs of our tribe. And then don't be afraid to enter in and sing along. On this third Sunday in Advent, listen for the Advent songs of Jesus, calling us into God's peaceable kingdom, where justice rolls down like water, and righteousness like an everlasting stream. Listen for the songs of our tribe, so that together we might be about the now and the not yet, participating in the creation of a world where wholeness, and rightness, and peace, are nothing less than the norm. Yes! Listen! Listen for the songs! For they are God's songs, and they are being sung throughout all creation!

Why Is There So Much Evil in The World?

January 22, 2017
(The Sunday after Trump's inauguration)

The days leading up to Trump's inauguration were as tumultuous as the months leading up to his election. One of his first actions was to sign an Executive Order attempting to repeal the Affordable Care Act, action which would ultimately be denied by Senator John McCain and the United States Senate. Clashes with the media continued, and the term 'fake news' made its entrance into the American vocabulary. Lying was becoming the norm for the administration, as counselor to the President Kellyanne Conway affirmed White House Press Secretary Sean Spicer's false claim that Trump had drawn the "largest audience ever to witness an inauguration."

On Saturday, the day following Trumps inauguration, and in response to misogynistic comments made by America's new president, our country experienced the largest single day protest in American history. The Women's March was a worldwide protest designed to advocate for women's rights, as well as immigration reform, racial equality, and countless other issues believed to be threatened because of the platform of the incoming administration. The DC march was the largest, with hundreds of thousands of participants. More than 3 million people participated in other marches around our country, and more than 7 million around the world.

The next two sermons were both part of a series titled "Questions of our Faith." Each question came from a member of our worshipping community, and both had remarkably relevant implications for many of the political issues dividing our nation.

Genesis 3:1-7
Now the serpent was more crafty than any other wild animal that the Lord God had made. He said to the woman, "Did God say, 'You shall not eat from any tree in the garden'?" The woman said to the serpent, "We may eat of the

fruit of the trees in the garden; but God said, 'You shall not eat of the fruit of the tree that is in the middle of the garden, nor shall you touch it, or you shall die.'" But the serpent said to the woman, "You will not die; for God knows that when you eat of it your eyes will be opened, and you will be like God, knowing good and evil." So when the woman saw that the tree was good for food, and that it was a delight to the eyes, and that the tree was to be desired to make one wise, she took of its fruit and ate; and she also gave some to her husband, who was with her, and he ate. Then the eyes of both were opened, and they knew that they were naked; and they sewed fig leaves together and made loincloths for themselves.

1 John 4:13-21

By this we know that we abide in him and he in us, because he has given us of his Spirit. And we have seen and do testify that the Father has sent his Son as the Savior of the world. God abides in those who confess that Jesus is the Son of God, and they abide in God. So we have known and believe the love that God has for us.

God is love, and those who abide in love abide in God, and God abides in them. Love has been perfected among us in this: that we may have boldness on the day of judgment, because as he is, so are we in this world. There is no fear in love, but perfect love casts out fear; for fear has to do with punishment, and whoever fears has not reached perfection in love. We love because he first loved us. Those who say, "I love God," and hate their brothers or sisters, are liars; for those who do not love a brother or sister whom they have seen, cannot love God whom they have not seen. The commandment we have from him is this: those who love God must love their brothers and sisters also.

So I have to confess that sometimes I feel like I enjoy my work too much to be paid for it! My wife, the bill payer in our family, doesn't always understand those sentiments; but for me they are very real!

I always love preaching, but I am especially enjoying all of the questions about our faith that were submitted Christmas Eve, and working on this series of sermons that seek to answer many of those questions. So I hope you are finding the resulting messages as meaningful as I am!

I also want to say by way of introduction that I am well aware that I do not have all of the definitive answers to all of the questions that people have about the mysteries of God, faith, and even the Church. Please know that I know that! My goal in this series is to simply lift up some of the important questions of our faith, to share some of the things that I have learned over the past 30 years in ministry; AND, I think most importantly, to perhaps give us all the freedom to dispel some of the rote and routine answers that have been given to these questions over the years – answers that simply no longer work, or that no longer make sense to a 21st century mind or to a 21st century faith.

This week's question is clearly the hardest of the five I've decided to deal with here in worship, and it's this: "Why is there so much evil in the world?" It is often referred to as the 'theodicy' question and has been asked for generations; because people in every day and age have experienced trials and tribulations and struggled to make sense of them. How, and why, does God allow them?

Such concerns were no doubt behind the writing of Genesis 3. In an attempt to describe reality, and the evil that abounds in our world, the writers' goal was likely to describe it, and to acknowledge its existence since the very beginning of time! Bad things have happened, and will continue to happen, all the time. Rain falls on the just and the unjust. And sometimes the laws of karma hold fast, and negative consequences for negative behavior do occasionally work themselves out. Sometimes blessings do come to those who live lives that bless others.

But this is not always the case. Far too often, evil, or that which is simply not of God, invades our world regardless of how we are living, and in spite of the God we claim to worship. Earthquakes rock continents. Disease invades our bodies. War devastates nations. Poverty strikes families and communities. And far too often all this occurs without regard for people's goodness, kindness, or faithfulness.

Randomness is a reality of the world in which we live. And when evil things make their way into our lives, all we can do is take a deep breath, link arms, and press on. In times of natural disaster we lean on first responders and aid workers. In times of sickness we turn to doctors and nurses. When financial hardships, or any hardship, strike, we trust that family and friends, neighbors and faith communities, will gather around us and walk with us through those dark nights of the soul. And we hope, and we trust, that we will land safely on the other side.

And that's life! The good comes with the bad: the weather of our lives includes sunny days as well as rainy ones, and sometimes evil walks hand in hand with blessing. It's what prompted the writer of Ecclesiastes to say that there is a time for every matter under the heavens: a time to laugh and to cry, to mend and to tear, to mourn and to dance, to war and to make peace – they are all two sides of the same coin, and nothing we can do in life is going to change that.

So it is understandable that sometimes evil does overwhelm us. Does it ever overwhelm you? I know it does me. This is particularly true when it comes to people harming, or hurting, other people. That is the evil I think that is being raised in this morning's question. That's the evil that is so disheartening . . . that is so . . . well, evil. Willful, intentional, conscious acts of cruelty simply lead me, and so many of us, to throw our hands up in the air and wonder where on earth is God. We don't understand why the evil isn't being destroyed, or why God isn't eliminating this debilitating reality.

And we do this, we cry out to God, because so many of us have been led to believe that God – a sovereign, omnipotent, omniscient, omnipresent being – in whom we have put our trust – and to whom we have given our very lives – this God should be able to change things. We cry out as if God doesn't already know of the pain and anguish of this world, and so he will know that somethings needs to be done. Where are you God? Why aren't you protecting us? Why aren't you saving us from all this evil?

We hint at this each week in the Lord's Prayer, asking to be delivered from evil. So? Why aren't be we being . . . delivered? Why does evil so often seem to be everywhere? Where is God when it's slimly tentacles are quietly wrapping themselves around the innocent, and threatening our very lives? Where is God?

And if these faulty ideas are bad enough, we've got more. How many have been taught that if we just accept the sovereign God, we will discover that the plans of the Divine are higher than ours, and way of the Holy are not like our ways! If we just accept Jesus into our lives and are baptized by the Holy Spirit, then we will be able to avoid the struggles that life wants to throw our way. We will learn to make better decisions and avoid the evil that comes from sinful living.

Oh, some are willing to accept that we will always have the occasional hurdle to get over; but by and large, God can be prayed to and the Spirit will take care of us. If we just learn to live better lives, more faithful and obedient lives, then God will take away the evil, and all will be well with our souls!

This is the way many of us are prone to want to read Genesis 3. God is the great cosmic punisher; and if we would just stop behaving badly, evil would cease to be, and God would take it all away. And we think this way because our minds can't reconcile the notion that God can exist alongside of evil. We want to believe that if God really is God, then surely evil could and should be eradicated from the face of the earth, or at the very least removed from the lives of faithful and obedient people.

But friends, what if all of this thinking about God is simply not very accurate? What if these concepts and ideas rest on a very flawed view of holiness, and divinity? That is the real crux of the question that is before us this morning.

We think that if God is, then evil shouldn't be – because God can and should be willing and able to conquer it. And so we don't allow ourselves to really wrestle with the fact that our lives, too often, don't reflect that great Easter proclamation – you know, about death, and evil, been swallowed up in victory. Death and evil too often still seem to abound, everywhere! And so when it appears that what we've been taught, what we've been led to believe, just doesn't make sense . . . well, rather than refining what we believe, we just throw it all out. And that is what so many have done with faith today. People are walking away from the Church every day, and never looking back; and more often than not it is because our teachings just don't make much sense.

But what if there is another way to think about these things? What if the time has come for us to find new answers to these old questions? What if God, or at the very least, our belief in God, does not rid the world of evil? What if, contrary to what many of us have been taught, God has chosen NOT, to be sovereign? What if God has chosen NOT, to be omnipotent? And as far as saying that God is omniscient – that God knows everything – the implication in that statement is that God thinks! But what if God isn't a thinking, or sentient being? What if God really is more like light, or love, than some kind of old man with a beard who reasons and rationalizes?

How many people today have thrown out the notion that God exists because they look at the brokenness of the world and say that if this is the world that God allows to exist, I want nothing to do with religion! If God truly is God they say, and can't solve all the problems of the world, then what kind of a God is this God that you worship and serve?

We're led to blame God for all the evil around us, when in fact WE are the ones deserving of the blame. For you see, God is not some kind of divine miracle worker, who like Bewitched, just twinkles her nose, and straightens everything out. God is not like some kind of a Genie in a Bottle, who nods her head, or snaps his fingers, and takes away our pain! Oh, God works. Yes. But not like that.

You see friends, as real as evil is, our faith is rooted in the idea that it never has the last word! In spite of the evil that exists in our world, the blessings of new life and resurrection reign! Tears tarry for the night, but joy DOES come in the morning. And in spite of the evil of our days, goodness does abound! There is far more peace in the world than there is war! Abundance shadows want! Life does triumph over death! And while none of that can minimizes the tragedy of war, want, or woe; it can serve as a powerful reminder that faithfulness always begs for perspective.

You see, what I'd like to put before us this morning is the realization that when God works, God works through us: through you and me. And if there's a little too much evil in the world for our liking, then let's not blame God, let's blame ourselves. Evil is not about God. The evil that can and should outrage all of us has absolutely nothing at all to do with God! Rather, it comes at the hands of women and men just like you and me. And that is the first thing that I want to put before us this morning.

My second point today is that far too often, this evil that WE create, and that WE condone, is all born in fear. This is what takes us to our second Scripture lesson; because more and more I am convinced that what leads people to evil acts, is fear: pure and simple! Fear demands a target. Whenever people are afraid, someONE has to be scapegoated, and evil is the result!

Think of the evil just in our lifetime! Nazism was born in a fear of the Jews. Apartheid in South Africa continued as long as it did because the white South African minority was fearful of the Black South African majority! McCarthyism, right here in America, was fueled by the fear of communism. Today, how much of the terrorism in our world is the result of religious peoples' fear of those who think or believe differently. And one must ask whether or not even the racism that we continue to struggle with in America does not trace its roots back to an inherent fear of those who simply look different than we do!

Why is there so much evil in the world?

Because people are so fearful!

We're afraid of Trumpers, and where we think they are going to take our country. We're afraid of people who wear pink hats, and the liberal agenda that they're trying to force upon us! We're afraid of Muslims, and what they're doing to what we thought was supposed to be a Christian country! We're afraid of immigrants, and all the crimes we're told they're committing. We're afraid of angry Blacks, racist cops, swamp-dwelling politicians, greedy corporate CEO's, biased news organizations, and on and on and on. Friends, where does it end?

Church, we do NOT need to be afraid. Fear will only paralyze and keep us from the work of God in this world. And if you were downtown at all these past three days or watched any of the events on TV then you have to know that. The inauguration of a new president reminded us of the power of the people. Yesterday's Women's March on Washington, and the related events around the world, should give EVERYONE hope that WE hold the future, in OUR hands!

You see, the greater question that is before us today, is what are we going to do with all the power that we have been given? Are we going to use it for good, or for evil?

Author WJ Dawson has said that "You need not choose evil; but have only to fail to choose good!" That's why there's so much evil today . . . not because of anything God has or has not done; but because too many of us, have chosen NOT to do good! Martin Luther King Jr. said that "Those who passively accept evil, are as much involved as those who perpetuate it!" He also said that in the end, we will remember not the words of our enemies, but the silence of our friends." Dietrich Bonhoeffer said that "Silence in the face of evil is itself, evil!" But I'm going to close this morning with the words of William Shakespeare, who said that "An evil person is like a dirty window. They never let the light shine through."

Yes! There is evil in this world. But it's not God's fault. It's our fault. And whatever God is going to do about evil, God is going to do thru us – people like you have me, who have the power to change everything. So let's keep speaking truth to power. Let's keep being the change that we want to see in this world. Let's push back against lies, and corruption, and the selfish abuse of power. Let's be God's ambassadors of peace, and let's never stop loving the unlovable.

And to God be all the glory . . . Amen!

Is Christianity Better Than Other Religions?

February 5, 2017

On January 27, 2017, during the first week of his presidency, Donald Trump issued Executive Order 13769, "Protecting the Nation from Foreign Terrorist Entry into the United State", often referred to as either the Muslim or Travel Ban. His intent was to limit the number of refugees admitted to the US, particularly the numbers of those coming from Syria and other predominantly Muslim countries.

Worship on this particular Sunday began with my reading the following "Call to Worship":

> Questions of our faith!
>
> Questions of our God!
>
> Today's world is full of questions that Christianity must be willing to answer. And that's what we've been trying to do the past few weeks. This morning, we tackle the fifth and final question – "Is Christianity better than other religions?"
>
> As you begin to consider YOUR answer to such a question; I invite you to do two things. First, in the spirit of the question before us today, we are going to be 'called to worship' by a singing bowl, common in the religions of the east, particularly Tibetan Buddhism. It may look very foreign to you, but it's nothing more than a standing bell, as opposed to a hanging bell. That's really the only difference. And whether in a Himalayan temple in Northern Nepal, or in Presbyterian Church in Alexandria, VA, the sound is meant to remind us of our need to take regular time to acknowledge the eternal presence of the holy one, in our lives, and in our world.

The second thing I want to invite you to do this morning is to close your eyes, take deep breathe, and let that eternal presence quiet within you any and every voice but the voice of this holy one – the Spirit of the living God.

Now, come friends, and let's worship.

John 10:11-16

"I am the good shepherd. The good shepherd lays down his life for the sheep. The hired hand, who is not the shepherd and does not own the sheep, sees the wolf coming and leaves the sheep and runs away—and the wolf snatches them and scatters them. The hired hand runs away because a hired hand does not care for the sheep. I am the good shepherd. I know my own and my own know me, just as the Father knows me and I know the Father. And I lay down my life for the sheep. I have other sheep that do not belong to this fold. I must bring them also, and they will listen to my voice. So there will be one flock, one shepherd.

Colossians 1:24-29

I am now rejoicing in my sufferings for your sake, and in my flesh, I am completing what is lacking in Christ's afflictions for the sake of his body, that is, the Church. I became its servant according to God's commission that was given to me for you, to make the word of God fully known, the mystery that has been hidden throughout the ages and generations but has now been revealed to his saints. To them God chose to make known how great among the Gentiles are the riches of the glory of this mystery, which is Christ in you, the hope of glory. It is he whom we proclaim, warning everyone and teaching everyone in all wisdom, so that we may present everyone mature in Christ. For this I toil and struggle with all the energy that he powerfully inspires within me.

Well I have to say that I'm sad this sermon series has come to an end. A topical series like this one has kept me from really delving into Scripture as much as I normally like to; but the questions we've considered over the past month have been good ones, important ones; and I hope you've all taken some time to really think them through, and to come up with your own answers to each of them. If you've missed any of the sermons and would like to catch up on them, they're all on the website (mvpconline.org) so feel free to check them out there.

This morning's final question, as I've already stated, has to do with whether or not Christianity is better than all the other religions of the world. But, before I share my thoughts on that question, I want to give you to the chance to do so. Now like so many questions related to our faith, and to God, there is not always a simple, black or white, yes or no, answer. I know that! But if pushed came to shove, and you could only answer yes, or no . . . how many of you would come down on the 'yes' side: and say that Christianity IS better that all the other world religions? And how many of you would land on the other side, and say NO, it's not?

In the end, I'm actually becoming more and more convinced that both answers are ok . . . as long as we have some qualifiers. And to explain what I mean, let me start with a short story.

Last Monday, Jeanne and I left for a Presbytery Retreat in Ocean City, NJ. Now as most of you know, any concept of heaven that I might be tempted to embrace is always going to involve sand and surf. The beach is where I experience God – you know that. And I did. I experienced God walking the boardwalk as the sun came up, listening to the sound of the waves, and just reflecting . . . on everything from family and faith, to marriage and ministry.

During our free time on Tuesday afternoon, a group of us went to see the movie "Lion", an Oscar nominated film about an Indian boy adopted by an Australian couple, who grows up and wants to find his roots back home. And I absolutely loved the film. It touched places deep inside of me and reminded me of issues and situations in my very own family. So as far as I'm concerned, I think it should win best film at this year's Academy Awards!

After the movie, we went to dinner at a great seafood restaurant. I ordered a delicious salmon special, with Brussel sprouts and roasted potatoes; while the woman next to me ordered chicken . . . at a seafood restaurant . . . at the beach.

Now the retreat was designed to provide an opportunity for the clergy and spouses in National Capital Presbytery to experience some rest, relaxation, and renewal, as we prepared for the upcoming Lenten season. And that is what most, if not all of us, experienced. But we all did it in different ways. While I was walking on the beach at 5:30 in the morning, other people, like my wife, were in bed. While I was listening New Testament scholar Francis Taylor Gench, from Union Seminary in Richmond, speak on the Gospel of John, others were in their rooms reading. While I was enjoying a movie about lostness and love, relationships and regrets, one of the women I know was off getting a pedicure. And while I was enjoying seafood, someone else was enjoying chicken.

And ya' know what? Regardless of our differing experiences, we all found the rest, relaxation, and renewal that we were seeking. Different means! Same end!

So do you know where I'm going?

Church, this is how we need to learn to begin to think about religion. When I bought my singing bowl, I told the guy behind the counter who I was and where the bowl was going to be used, and he pointed me to sign behind the counter that said, "All Juice, No Container!"

And I looked at him, puzzled, and he said, "God is like orange juice, religion is just the container!"

And I smiled and said to him, "We sure do love containers don't we?"

Friends, maturity of faith involves moving beyond the simplistic and misguided idea that faith is about belief systems, judged according to one's individual standards of right or wrong, good or bad, true or false. Instead, as revealed by Jesus himself, our faith, and any faith, always and only needs to be measured by the fruit that is being born. That's it.

And the writer of John 10 seems to know this. The writer of the Gospel According to John seems to know that there are indeed people of other folds, also seeking the things of God, in other places, in other parts of the world, in other religions. And those people are not the enemy. They are our brothers and our sisters. John seems to know that Jesus' way is a way that is being sought by many different people, and regardless of what that 'way' is called, it can and does bring people into union with all that is holy. Apparently, the Jews are *not* the only people to be considered "the apple of God's eye"! Apparently, the writer of John knows that in this great big world, there are all kinds of paths that have the capacity to lead people toward God. And as long as those paths reflect the ways of Jesus, then they need not be feared.

In Colossians, the author follows a similar path, making it clear that Jesus didn't just come for the Jews! Jesus' life was about revealing the mysteries of God to the Gentile community as well; and communicating this reality is what was at the heart of the ministry of the Apostle Paul. Again and again Paul's message was that Jesus came for everyone; which is why both of the passages we read this morning reveal that ours is a God who draws circles that INclude, rather than lines designed to EXclude. Here that again. Jesus, and the life to which each one of us is called, is not about drawing boundaries that wall people out. Ours is a faith that seek to build communities of inclusion that invite people in – all people, everywhere!

Now, I would guess that most of us here know that. I think it's accurate for me to presume that MOST of us here at Mt. Vernon KNOW . . . that rather than being right and believing that all the other religions of the world are wrong; we are here because this Jesus thing just works well for us. It makes sense, for us; and our experiences in the Christian Church truly HAVE brought our faith to life. It's why we're here. That's why some of us answered 'yes' to my initial question. For us, and there's the qualifier, Christianity IS better than all the other religions of the world. But that qualifier is key! Christianity is better than all the other religions of the world . . . for me . . . for us! And while nothing moves me closer to God than the cross of Jesus, I can still value other bells that call me to worship, and other images that move me toward holiness!

Early morning walks are better than sleeping until noon – for me! And seafood is better than chicken – for me. Such statements are MY truths; but they're not the only truths! And that is perhaps what led some of you to say that 'no', Christianity is NOT better than other religions. For lots of people have found great meaning in life without ever even uttering the name of Jesus, and the fruit that they bear has still managed to move them, and point others, toward God.

Friends, there is a common thread that runs through all the major religions of the world. And that thread is the thread of love. That is the way of Jesus, and it's the only way that really matters. And it's in Islam, and Judaism, and Buddhism. It's everywhere. And so rather that continually trying to convert people to our way of thinking and believing, maybe, just maybe, we need to simply grab that common thread, and allow it to bind us together, and to knit our hearts into the one heart, beating in love, for this great human family of which we are all a part!

And Church, this is realization is more critical today than ever! I don't know where you are when it comes to the state of our nation, or our world; but I think it's a mess. I have never seen people as polarized as we are today . . . about everything. And we don't just disagree, we go to war with one another over our differences. And the only thing that is going to be able to change this, is that common thread that runs through each and every faith community around the world. We Christians can't do it alone. We need one another.

In addition to spending the first part of last week at a Presbytery Retreat, I spent the end of the week at a Sister Giant conference, in Crystal City; and it was a powerful reminder of the unity that people of all faiths, can, and must, begin to focus on.

On Friday morning there was a panel discussion that included author Diana Butler Bass representing the white Christian church; James Forbes, the former pastor of NY City's Riverside Church representing the Black Christian community; Harris Tarin, the Afghan-American Muslim Director of the Washington DC office of the Muslim Public Affairs Council; Cat Zavis, a Jewish attorney who is currently serving as the Executive Director of the Network of Spiritual Progressives; and Robert Thurman, and American Buddhist writer and the co-founder and president of the Tibet House in NYC.

All five participants were passionate, and brilliant women and men, deeply committed and devoted to their respective traditions, but who also knew at the core of their being, that such commitment and devotion brought them into a very deep sense of oneness and unity with one another: not just with God, but WITH ONE ANOTHER. They were not enemies! They were friends; and they knew that faithfulness is not about which religion is better or worse. Faithfulness is about love – loving God and loving others. And that is the only thing that is going to change our world. For without love, we're never going to be able to come to together. And that does not mean being quiet; or not having passion, and conviction; or a commitment to that which is good and right. But it does mean that we have to learn to respect one another and work together and see beyond all of our differences, differences that many would like to use to keep us divide from one another. It means we have to dig a little bit and discover the common ground upon which so many of us are standing. It means we need to stop condemning what other people believe, because far too often we don't even really know what other people believe.

20th century Swedish author, theologian and New Testament scholar Krister Stendhal, who served as the Dean of the Divinity School at Harvard University in the 70s and 80s, crafted what has become known as the Three Rules of Religious Understanding; and I share them this morning in the hopes that they might help all of us do a better job of understanding the faith of those whose beliefs are different from our own.

1) When trying to understand another religion, you should ask the adherents of that religion and not the religion's enemies! Just as we wouldn't send the world to Richard Dawkins, author of the 2006 book "The God Delusion", to learn about Christianity; neither should we be learning about the various faiths of the world from anyone but those who practices those various faiths.

2) We can't compare the best of our religion, to the worst of another religion! And this is why so many of us today are so concerned about NOT allowing the radical terrorists around the world to become the spokespeople for the religions they claim to embrace. The terrorist who shoots up a nightclub in Paris doesn't represent the Muslim faith any more than the terrorist who shoots up a Mosque in Quebec City represents the Christian faith. And finally,

3) Leave room for, or I would say learn to develop, something called "holy envy"! And the best example I can offer comes from a conversation I had with a friend I had dinner with last weekend. The guy has been doing a great deal of work with the schools in the United Arab Emirate of Dubai! Now because it is an Arab country, five times a day, he hears the Muslim call to prayer; and he was sharing with me how at first, it was rather disconcerting. But over time, he said, particularly during his morning runs, often under a crescent moon, it became a comfort, and a welcome intrusion to his day – a reminder to stop, and be still, and simply remember that God is on God's throne, regardless of all that is going on in the world around us.

Friends, other religions have much to teach us. And if we'd all learn to pool our wisdom, and knowledge, and understanding, together, perhaps we really might be able to change this world.

Author and spiritualist Marianne Williams was one of the hosts of the Sister Giant Conference, and more than once she said, "Hatred has a perverse kind of courage."

We all need to remember the truth embedded in that powerful statement. Hating others, for whatever reason, grows within us the capacity to commit unspeakable evil.

But love? Love changes everything. And love is at the heart of the God revealed in Jesus. It's a love mandated in the Hadith, a collection of the most important teachings of Muhammed. It's a love that the Buddha says nourishes the soul as blood nourishes the heart.

We Christians are prone to want to think that because we are the largest religion in the world, that we have the corner on the market of goodness, and rightness, and love. We have a history that reveals a desire to get everyone to think and believe the way we think and believe. And we are tempted every day to believe that not only is our faith better than all other religions, but that other religions are actually evil!

As we come to this table this morning, may this be our confession; and may God's forgiveness lead us to work not just for *Christian* unity, but for unity among *all* faithful people, of every religion, all around this great big world that we call home.

And to God be the glory, Amen!

Shhh! Don't Tell! I'm Not Sure I Believe in God!

June 25, 2017

On Monday of this week, a driver plowed his van into a crowd of people outside of North London Mosque, killing one person and injuring eight others; and closer to home, in my home-state of Virginia, a 17-year-old Muslim girl was killed on her way home from evening prayer services.

As the reality of the Trump's presidency sets in – a reality where blatant and childish lies, narcissistic and selfish goals, divisive and erratic tweets, and slanderous and aggressive name-calling have become the norm – the Church becomes a place of refuge from a tragically broken political system. While evangelical Christianity refuses to acknowledge the political sins being condoned on a daily basis, thus contributing to the American Church's ongoing loss of credibility at home and abroad, many Presbyterian are showing up for worship on Sunday morning in order to find a modicum of hope, encouragement, and peace. They are looking for clarity with regard to what it means to truly follow Jesus, to resist evil, and to partner with the Spirit's work in the world.

This sermon was part of a series on secrets, and on this particular Sunday our community sang a Jane Parker Huber hymn: "Called as Partners in Christ's Service."

> *Called as partners in Christ's service, called to ministries of grace,*
> *We respond with deep commitment, fresh new lines of faith to trace.*
>
> *May we learn the art of sharing side by side and friend with friend,*
> *Equal partners in our caring to fulfill God's chosen end.*
>
> *Christ's example, Christ's inspiring, Christ's clear call to work and worth,*
> *Let us follow never faltering, reconciling folk on earth.*
>
> *Men and women, richer, poorer, all God's people young and old,*
> *Blending human skills together gracious gifts of God unfold.*

Thus new patterns for Christ's mission, in a small or global sense,
Help us bear each other's burdens, breaking down each wall or fence.

Words of comfort, words of vision, words of challenge said with care,
Bring new power and strength for action, make us colleagues free and fair.

So God grant us for tomorrow ways to order human life
That surrounds each person sorrow with a calm that conquers strife.

Make us partners in our living, our compassion to increase,
Messengers thus giving hope, and confident, and peace.

Luke 15:11-24

Then Jesus said, "There was a man who had two sons. The younger of them said to his father, 'Father, give me the share of the property that will belong to me.' So he divided his property between them. A few days later the younger son gathered all he had and traveled to a distant country, and there he squandered his property in dissolute living. When he had spent everything, a severe famine took place throughout that country, and he began to be in need. So he went and hired himself out to one of the citizens of that country, who sent him to his fields to feed the pigs. He would gladly have filled himself with the pods that the pigs were eating; and no one gave him anything. But when he came to himself he said, 'How many of my father's hired hands have bread enough and to spare, but here I am dying of hunger! I will get up and go to my father, and I will say to him, "Father, I have sinned against heaven and before you; I am no longer worthy to be called your son; treat me like one of your hired hands."' So he set off and went to his father. But while he was still far off, his father saw him and was filled with compassion; he ran and put his arms around him and kissed him. Then the son said to him, 'Father, I have sinned against heaven and before you; I am no longer worthy to be called your son.' But the father said to his slaves, 'Quickly, bring out a robe—the best one—and put it on him; put a ring on his finger and sandals on his feet. And get the fatted calf and kill it and let us eat and celebrate; for this son of mine was dead and is alive again; he was lost and is found!' And they began to celebrate."

Luke 15:25-32

"Now (the loving father's) elder son was in the field; and when he came and approached the house, he heard music and dancing. He called one of the slaves

and asked what was going on. He replied, 'Your brother has come, and your father has killed the fatted calf, because he has got him back safe and sound.' Then he became angry and refused to go in. His father came out and began to plead with him. But he answered his father, 'Listen! For all these years I have been working like a slave for you, and I have never disobeyed your command; yet you have never given me even a young goat so that I might celebrate with my friends. But when this son of yours came back, who has devoured your property with prostitutes, you killed the fatted calf for him!' Then the father[a] said to him, 'Son, you are always with me, and all that is mine is yours. But we had to celebrate and rejoice, because this brother of yours was dead and has come to life; he was lost and has been found.'"

I get it! At least I think I do!

I've spent enough time with NONES, and DONES; with millennials who want nothing to do with institutional religion, as well as with Boomers and Busters who have simply given up on it; I've spent enough time with all of them . . . to get it!

We've simply let them down. We've perpetuated antiquated and outdated beliefs, all in the name of tradition, and in so doing we've become tragically irrelevant. We've pit science against faith, and made it appear as though one can't be an intelligent, thinking person, and still love Jesus. And we've been hypocritical in our lifestyles, substituting patriotism and personal morality for kindness and compassion. As a result, we've not just failed ourselves and our churches, but we've failed God. And I get it! When people say that the Church appears to be giving the world a choice between ignorance on fire, or wisdom on ice – I get it!

Thursday morning, after a couple hours in Starbucks working on this sermon, and before a 10:30 meeting, I met with a friend from my college days. I've mentioned him before. In August it will be 36 years since we met, and we still enjoy getting together to talk about God, the church, love, and our faith journeys. And while this friend is neither a NONE, nor a DONE, like so many of us, he too struggles to move beyond an image of God and faithfulness that seems to deny the very Christ that we see in the Gospel. The image that Luke is seeking to paint for us in this morning's readings, in what is perhaps one of the most well-known Biblical parables, is simply very different from the image of God that is being painted for us by so many religious institutions in general, and by the Christian Church in specific. For far too often, the pictures that we have today are being painted by religious extremists; and their loud, boisterous, attention-grabbing voices, should frighten all of us.

These days, when it comes to the world stage, the most vocal and well-known expression of so-called "religious faithfulness" is radical, Islamic extremism. In what can be described as nothing less than a gross distortion of the Muslim faith, misguided and misled terrorists have tragically distorted and misrepresented the essential teachings of the world's second largest religion. Setting off bombs in train stations and driving cars into crowds of people, all because one believes that is what god demands, is nothing short of absurd, and it in no way reflects a healthy understanding of either God or the Islamic tradition. Which is why such pictures of holiness and faithfulness need to be boldly and bluntly rejected; and those who would continue to push and promulgate such ideas must be called out.

But we all know this, right? We all know that these people need to be challenged and that the faith they proclaim needs to be rejected. So this morning let's move a little closer to home, ok? Because while radical, Islamic extremists may be one of the world's greatest problems in 2017; here in America, some would say that our greatest problem is radical, CHRISTIAN extremism.

Why certainly far less physically violent that the Muslim extremist, Christian extremists are those who would still have us believe that women are to be under the authority of men; that God hates homosexuality; that those who do not embrace correct belief are destined to an eternity in a place where there is weeping and gnashing of teeth; and that America was founded as a beacon of light for all the world, and thus needs to remain Christian, AND white – for that is God's desire. Their literalistic approach to Scripture has led to the creation of a very distorted and frightening view of the world: where everything has been pre-ordained, and where when we attempt to violate God's will, God steps in to punish offenders . . . and harshly! These people believe that God is so holy, and so set apart, that He . . . and yes, God is HE . . . He is so holy and set apart that He cannot look upon human sin. As the 'story' then goes, God requires the shedding of blood in order to forgive the brokenness of humanity: thus, the story of Jesus! To this day, such extremists further contend that that because people continue to stray, God doesn't merely use, but actually sends, natural disasters, national calamities, and personal tragedies – all to teach and instruct, to reprimand and restore, to punish and to purify.

So with these two extremes before us, is it any wonder that NONES, and DONES abound today? Both Muslim extremists around the world, and Christian extremists right here at home, are not only misrepresenting their respective faith traditions, and actually deterring people from finding the hope, and meaning, and fellowship, that their respective traditions can provide; but they are also distorting peoples' understanding of God. And this is what leads me to include a sermon like this in a series on things we tend to hide.

You see, at least when it comes to American Christianity, studies have indicated again and again that people have rightly begun to move away from the antiquated notion of an angry, vengeful, and malicious God. Many of us have begun to embrace an ever-growing and maturing, reformed and constantly reforming understanding of God. But sadly, we are all too often afraid to speak up and say anything. We have all kinds of questions about some of things that we've been taught about God, but we try to hide them. We don't ask our questions about those things that concern us; and such hiding inhibits the community that should exist within the Body of Christ. People are left thinking that there's something wrong with them because they can no longer accept the teachings of the religious extremists today. And because there is not a forum to discuss such things, and because the church almost appears to be afraid of the questions, we give the impression that we just don't get it! The people outside of our walls think the extremists speak for all of us; and that anyone who has questions is not welcome. They conclude there is no room for them; and throwing out the baby with the bathwater they walk away from our churches, never to return!

It's what leads people to say to me all the time, "Ya' know Pastor Bob, I'm just not sure I even believe in God anymore." To which my response is always, and some of you have heard me say this: "Tell me about this god that you don't believe in, because I'm not sure I believe in that kind of a god either!"

Church, it's OK to challenge, and to question, and to wrestle with some of this Body's traditional teachings. God can handle it. Your faith can handle it. In fact I would bet that we, both individual, and corporately, would in the end, wind up being stronger, if we just gave one another a little space, a little room to breathe, when it comes to our experiences of and with God. If we all would just stop hiding all of our questions, doubts, and uncertainties, perhaps, just perhaps, the trajectory of religious institutions around the world might change. And friends, I am more and more convinced that this process can begin when we begin to embrace a picture of God like the one given to us by Luke in this morning's story of the Prodigal Son and the Loving Father.

What Luke is attempting to show us in today's readings is that God is not angry or vengeful. Consider the story. The rebel son asks his father for his inheritance, and then goes and blows it all on wild living. He goes to the big city in search of new and exciting experiences. He heads out west to find himself. He goes . . . backpacking around Europe to figure out what he wants to do with his life. It really is an age-old story, isn't it; and we get it. We all know how it ends.

The young man blows all his money, can't afford to even buy food so he can eat, and winds up taking a job . . . feeding pigs. He 'finds himself' alright, and he discovers really quickly what he DOESN'T want to do with his life. He begins this spiral downward, and eventually comes to a place where he realizes that there is only one thing for him to do. And that is to go home. He comes to his senses, realizes that he made a terrible mistake, and that they only place for him to go now, is home! So that's what he does.

And when he does, we catch this beautiful glimpse of the very nature and character of God!

Look at how this rebel son greeted.

Luke tells us that "while he was still far off, his father saw him and was filled with compassion; AND HE RAN . . . put his arms around him . . . kissed him . . . and welcomed him home!"

Folks this is the picture of God that the world so desperately needs today – a picture of a God running to it, eager to welcome it, and to embrace it, and to even kiss it and welcome it . . . home! What a contrast: God, running to all the peoples of the world, and not to judge them, or to condemn them, but to embrace them.

In the story, the son doesn't even get the chance to apologize. In fact he doesn't get to say a thing. All his father sees is a long-lost child making his way back home. And so he runs! What a beautiful image! It doesn't matter where you've been, or what you've done: God is running toward you to embrace you, and to welcome you!

This morning, if you are hiding doubts about a God who you've been taught is more interested in scolding than in saving, then hear this message. You can stop hiding . . . because you're not alone . . . at least not here at Mt. Vernon Pres! We're with you. We . . . get it. And there is indeed another way to think about, and to talk about, faith, and religion, and God.

Philips, Craig, and Dean is a group that has been around for a while. But they have a song that I think speaks as powerfully today as it did when it was first released back in 1999. They too seem to get it. Listen to these words from their song, "When God Ran."

> *Almighty God, The Great I Am,*
> *Immovable Rock, Omnipotent, Powerful,*
> *Awesome Lord.*
> *Victorious Warrior, Commanding King of Kings,*
> *Mighty Conqueror . . . and the only time,*
> *The only time I ever saw him run,*
> *Was when*
> *He ran to me,*
> *He took me in His arms,*
> *Held my head to His chest,*

Said "My son's come home again!"
Lifted my face,
Wiped the tears from my eyes,
With forgiveness in His voice He said
"Son, do you know I still love You?"
He caught me by surprise, When God ran
The day I left home,
I knew I'd broken His heart.
And I wondered then, if things could ever be the same.
Then one night,
I remembered His love for me.
And down that dusty road, ahead I could see,
It was the only time,
It was the only time I ever saw Him run.
And then
He ran to me,
He took me in His arms,
Held my head to His chest,
Said "My son's come home again!"
Lifted my face,
Wiped the tears from my eyes,
With forgiveness in His voice He said
"Son, do you know I still love You?"
He said "Son". He called me Son.
He ran to me. And then I ran to Him

Friends, as you reflect on those lyrics, let me ask you a question. Do you . . . get it? The God we worship is a God who runs . . . to each of us! That's what we see in Jesus. It's what Luke is trying to tell us. And the messed-up picture of the extremists in the world today – just know it is not accurate. And we not only CAN question it, we MUST question it. All of us! Because it's simply not true!

The Great I Am, the Immovable Rock, our awesome Lord . . . runs to each of us. Just as all loving parents, who take us in their arms, and hold our heads to their chests, and say "my child is home": so too does God! And lifting our faces, wiping the tears from our eyes, and with great forgiveness, our God says, "Do you know how much I love you?"

This is the picture of God that is so needed today – around the world, and right here at home. So however you understand God – whether as some kind of sentient being, who thinks and reasons just like you and I; or whether more like a force, moving all creation towards that which is right and good, kind and loving – however you understand God, know that there is no room in that picture for violence, hatred, or injustice.

It's about time we get it, don't you think? For the future of our world is depending upon it.

The Gospel According to the Beatles
August 13 and August 20, 2017

The sermon that I have included here is actually a combination of two different sermons, so it is a little longer than usual! Both of them were preached in August of 2017, on the two Sundays following the "Unite the White Rally" in Charlottesville, VA. The rally was in response to a movement around the country seeking to remove Confederate monuments that have been erected on public land all across America; and the violence that erupted led to a White Supremacist killing a young woman by the name of Heather Heyer and injuring nearly 40 others. But the most tragic aspect of the weekend was our President's response to all the hatred and violence. Failing to condemn the racist actions of the supremacists, and with words that will likely echo for years to come, Trump proclaimed "there were good people on both sides."

1 Thessalonians 5:1-11

Now concerning the times and the seasons, brothers and sisters, you do not need to have anything written to you. For you yourselves know very well that the day of the Lord will come like a thief in the night. When they say, "There is peace and security," then sudden destruction will come upon them, as labor pains come upon a pregnant woman, and there will be no escape! But you, beloved, are not in darkness, for that day to surprise you like a thief; for you are all children of light and children of the day; we are not of the night or of darkness. So then let us not fall asleep as others do but let us keep awake and be sober; for those who sleep, sleep at night, and those who are drunk, get drunk at night. But since we belong to the day, let us be sober, and put on the breastplate of faith and love, and for a helmet the hope of salvation. For God has destined us not for wrath but for obtaining salvation through our Lord Jesus Christ, who died for us, so that whether we are awake or asleep we may live with him. Therefore encourage one another and build up each other, as indeed you are doing.

Ephesians 4:1-16

I therefore, the prisoner in the Lord, beg you to lead a life worthy of the calling to which you have been called, with all humility and gentleness, with patience, bearing with one another in love, making every effort to maintain the unity of the Spirit in the bond of peace. There is one body and one Spirit, just as you were called to the one hope of your calling, one Lord, one faith, one baptism, one God and Father of all, who is above all and through all and in all. But each of us was given grace according to the measure of Christ's gift. Therefore it is said, "When he ascended on high, he made captivity itself a captive; he gave gifts to his people." (When it says, "He ascended," what does it mean but that he had also descended into the lower parts of the earth? He who descended is the same one who ascended far above all the heavens, so that he might fill all things.) The gifts he gave were that some would be apostles, some prophets, some evangelists, some pastors and teachers, to equip the saints for the work of ministry, for building up the body of Christ, until all of us come to the unity of the faith and of the knowledge of the Son of God, to maturity, to the measure of the full stature of Christ. We must no longer be children, tossed to and fro and blown about by every wind of doctrine, by people's trickery, by their craftiness in deceitful scheming. But speaking the truth in love, we must grow up in every way into him who is the head, into Christ, from whom the whole body, joined and knit together by every ligament with which it is equipped, as each part is working properly, promotes the body's growth in building itself up in love.

In addition to this being our first Sunday in our remodeled worship space, this is also my first Sunday here after some vacation, and it is good to be back with you. I always love going away, but I always love coming home. And as I've already indicated in my children's sermon, I think of you while I'm gone more than you probably realize.

As I hope you all know, I am a husband and a father before I am a pastor, and so I'm grateful for all the vacation time that you give me. I don't take it for granted; and over the next few weeks I am going to try to work into my sermons some of the things that I did, and saw, and experienced. AND, I'm going to try and to do it in a new sermon series titled "The Gospel According to the Beatles."

Now I have to confess right at the outset this morning that I'm not much of a Beatles fan. But my wife and daughter are, and so when I saw a book by this very title at General Assembly last year in Portland, I couldn't resist. So as the summer begins to draw to a close, we're going to consider the Gospel as it comes to us in what some might consider to be a less than orthodox manner: from the Beatles, beginning this morning with the song you just heard, released on August 6, 1965 – 52 years ago last Sunday. "Help" was written by John Lennon, and originally meant to be a ballad, not the up-tempo pop song that it became as a result of all kinds of commercial pressure. And while it may not be one of their most successful singles, it is a great way to kick off this series because it is this cry of the human heart to which the Gospel responds: Help!

I won't even begin to presume to know what these four men thought about Jesus; but I think their lives bear testimony to the fact that as they got older, they actually displayed at the very least, a growing spirituality. And I say that because of songs like this one. Hear again John's lyrics:

> *Help! I need somebody*
> *Help! Not just anybody*
> *Help! You know I need someone*
> *Help!*
>
> *When I was younger, so much younger than today*
> *I never needed anybody's help in any way*
> *But now these days are gone and I'm not so self-assured*
> *Now I find I've changed my mind; I've opened up the doors*
>
> *Help me if you can, I'm feeling down*
> *And I do appreciate you being 'round*

Help me get my feet back on the ground
Won't you please, please help me?

And now my life has changed in oh so many ways
My independence seems to vanish in the haze
But ev'ry now and then I feel so insecure
I know that I just need you like I've never done before

Help me if you can, I'm feeling down
And I do appreciate you being 'round
Help me get my feet back on the ground
Won't you please, please help me?

How many times have you heard me preach on our need for one another? Because "it is not good for us to be alone," acknowledging our need for one another is critical to any living and vibrant faith. Companionship, that both cares FOR others and receives care FROM others, is what knits us together – body, soul, and spirit! It's what prompted the writer of Thessalonians to say in this morning's first passage: "speak encouraging words to one another. Build up hope so you'll all be together in this . . . no one left out, no one left behind."

And friends, if any words need to be spoken loudly and boldly today, it is these . . . from Eugene Peterson's translation, in The Message ". . . NO ONE LEFT OUT . . . NO ONE LEFT BEHIND!"

Listen to how he translates parts of the second passage we read this morning: "Here's what I want you to do . . . I want you to get out there and walk—better yet, run! —on the road God called you to travel. I don't want any of you sitting around on your hands. I don't want anyone strolling off, down some path that goes nowhere. And mark that you do this with humility and discipline—not in fits and starts, but steadily, pouring yourselves out for each other in acts of love, alert at noticing differences and quick at mending fences. You were all called to travel on the same road and in the same direction, so stay together, both outwardly and inwardly . . . (This) doesn't mean you should all look and speak and act the same. Out of the generosity of Christ, each of us is given his own gift . . . to train Christ's followers in skilled servant work, working within Christ's body, the church, until we're all moving rhythmically and easily with each other, efficient and graceful in response to God's Son, fully mature adults, fully developed within and without, fully alive like Christ. No prolonged infancies among us, please. We'll not tolerate babes in the woods, small children who are an easy mark for impostors. God wants us to grow up, to know the whole truth and tell it in love—like Christ in everything. We take our lead from Christ, who is the source of everything we do. He keeps us in step with each other. His very breath and blood flow through us, nourishing us so that we will grow up healthy in God, robust in love."

What more really needs to be said? This is the Gospel. And a song like "Help" reveals Lennon's knowledge of this profound human need. Paraphrasing another passage, the eye cannot say to the foot I don't need you. Life was meant to be lived in community, because we all have different gifts, and abilities, skills, and talents. And we, this body called the Church – WE are called to model how to do this for the world, caring for others while at the same time allowing others to care for us.

Now since I don't think a sermon is really a sermon unless it pushes us a little bit, here's today's challenge. We white, middle and upper middle-class Americans are generally pretty good at caring for others. Not always, but most of us here strive to do this all the time. We're not perfect, but we're trying.

However while we take seriously Christ's call to care for the least of these, we're not always very good at allowing others care for us.

We, albeit often unconsciously, submit to the white savior complex, believing that it's our job to rescue the world. But as far as learning to let others do for us, that's a different story; a different song, if you will. I've given you this challenge before, I know; but this Beatles song forces me to life it up again today. Who cares for you? Who are you vulnerable with? Who do you allow to know your needs, so that they might care for you? With whom are you able to let your guard down, and drop your defenses, so that you might be seen for who you really are – a person with needs just like everyone else? Who has heard your cries . . . for help!

This is one of the most important fruits of small group ministry. It's wonderful to enjoy one another's company, and to read and study together; but might our groups become a little more than that? Might they become places where we are learning to open up to one another about all that is going on in our lives so that real and genuine intimacy might be developed?

Perhaps because of all the pressures of fame and fortune, John Lennon knew that he needed others in his life. Clearly, he was well aware that independence wasn't all it's often cracked up to be, and that keeping his feet on the ground required . . . help.

But how about us? Do we?

If so, then let's . . . help . . . one another, and make sure that no one is left out, that no one is left behind.

This was where my sermon ended last Thursday. But then Friday came, and hundreds of members of various hate groups - the KKK, Neo-Nazis, and White Supremacists, all of whom are part of the new alt-right in America - descended upon Charlottesville, a quintessential Virginia town, full of history, and home to one of our nation's most well-respected public universities.

When darkness fell, young, white men, carrying torches, reminiscent of Nazi marches in Germany in the 1930s, and KKK rallies right here in the Old Dominion in the 1950s and 60s, moved in. On Saturday, these same people, hundreds of them, rallied in the quiet town with guns, baseball bats, and hate-filled speech, condemning Jews, Blacks, and other minority groups, all in an attempt to fulfill the promises of outrageous and extreme political figures who desire to take us back to the good 'old days, when America was Christian, white, and pure!

Well friends, today, the city of Charlottesville, the state of Virginia, and this nation that we call home, are all crying out for help. And as the Church of Jesus Christ, we simply cannot sit by, and silently close our eyes to an injustice that we believe we've put behind us, but that has in fact become institutionalize that many don't even see it.

We are living in a nation where more and more people are crying out for . . . help. For far too many ARE being left out and left behind. They need help from somebody; and friends, as the Church of Jesus Christ, the risen body of Christ in the world today, that somebody is us!

Elie Wiesel once said, "there may be times when we are powerless to prevent injustice; but there must never be a time when we fail to protest it." And why is this so true? Because in the words of another Beatles hit, our world is full of lonely people: people with unimaginable need. And the evils of injustice are ravaging places near and far. So we in the Church have no choice but to act.

One of the first things I did when I arrived here 4 years ago was to remove the corporate prayer of confession from our weekly worship gatherings. And as I've explained to many of you, I did that NOT because I don't think sin is real, or because I don't take seriously it's destructive power; but because I no longer believe that our primary identity in the eyes of God is that of a sinner. However, over the past year, the brokenness of our world has overwhelmed me. Charlottesville, the President's response, and a recent experience with White Supremacist and Nazi-Sympathizer Richard Spencer, are all leading me, and others, to decide that we can no longer remain silent.

So let me tell you about this Mr. Spencer.

Last week my wife and I attended a small, and seemingly insignificant protest, outside of his office, in Old Town Alexandria. Now we don't normally do things like that, but these are not normal days!

In case you don't know, Spencer was one of the organizers of the Unite the Right Rally, and as the self-proclaimed founder of the Alt-Right, he travels the nation promoting his bigoted worldview. So when we heard about this silent, candlelight vigil, we headed out. It was time to take a public stand against racism, and against hatred, and to truly "stand on the side of love."

But what happened . . . well to say it surprised me would be the understatement of my week, maybe my year. I was simply astonished by the events that took place; for on the corner of King and Patrick Streets, with 30 or so other saints, my wife and I looked evil in the eye. In what was a truly transformative experience, unlike any I can remember, we encountered a hatred that we'd never really seen before, at least not so up close and personal.

Spencer chose to come down from his office and to walk among our group; and so right there, on a street, and in a town, that I've grown to love so much, standing in front of me, not much more than a foot from my face, in the glowing light of my candle, I looked into the eyes of real evil. And I don't say that lightly, because I know how harsh it sounds. But in his eyes, I saw so much hatred that I felt dirty when he finally walked away.

Now surprisingly, I wasn't angry. Contrary to my nature, I didn't want to argue with him, or debate him. I didn't want to yell at him or hit him. None of that! Surprisingly, all I felt was sadness . . . deep, deep sadness . . . disbelief that anyone could possibly harbor so much hatred in their heart and be so evil! Perhaps because of some small-town, sheltered naiveté, or perhaps because of what I can only hope to be a constantly growing Christlikeness, my heart broke. Because in his eyes, all I could see was anger and animosity, meanness and malice, hatred and hubris. And it just saddened me in a way I don't think I've ever been saddened before. And I don't mean to sound overly dramatic; but at that very moment, something in me clicked. Something happened.

Needless to say I didn't sleep well that night, and I spent most of the next day reading, and writing, and trying to figure out what God was saying to me, what Spirit of God was doing in me, and to me. Around 12:30 I decided to go to Starbucks for lunch, and while I was waiting in line for Nicolas, the barista on duty that afternoon, to stop what he was doing to take my order, a middle-aged lady waltzed in, cut in front of me, and began shouting her order to whoever was supposed to be listening. Now Nicholas watched it all happen, and just looked at me and smiled.

Again, surprisingly, I didn't say anything to the woman, even though many of you know I'm that kind of guy. Instead, I just held out my hand, and let her go ahead and order. I thought, and even said to Nicolas a few minutes later, there are far more important issues for us to be concerned about today that a lady being rushed and needing to get in and out of Starbucks quickly.

Now lest you're inclined to think "Oh my, don't we have a wonderful pastor!" – allow me to set you straight. While I know well how to wear the pastoral mantle, I'm human, just like you. No, I'm not a bad person, but . . . I use my car horn way too much; and when people cut in front of me, probably like you, I'm usually quick to call them out. But on Tuesday? . . . on Tuesday I just couldn't. I was still lost in the hatred that I'd seen the night before.

Before the woman could even walk out of the door, Nicholas, was apologizing, and said to me "What are you having today – it's on the house. That was really kind of you not to say anything."

I'm not exaggerating when I tell you that I almost started crying right there at the register. It makes me want to cry right now, and I don't really even know why. Except to say that I think I'm finally beginning to discover, and to understand, what I've probably been preaching for a long time. And that is that all of us have choices to make in this life. And those choices can either lead to love, or they can lead to hate.

So, beginning today, I want mine to be for love . . . as often as possible!

I think I've probably spent close to ALL of my 56 years thinking that it was my job to not only make this choice for myself; but I think I've also believed that it was my job to convince, and convert, and coax, and cajole, and compel others to make this very same choice that I am seeking to make. But as many of you know, that is just exhausting and frustrating and maddening and disappointing and discouraging. Some people are just filled with too much hate. They are miserable, contrarian, nasty people. They are never going to hear what we have to say. And I've come to believe that's what Jesus meant when he talked about people having 'ears to hear.' I think it's also what he meant when he told us not to cast our pearls before swine. A friend of mine once told me that not everyone is always able to hear, what we are called to say! They're not at a place where they can take it in, grasp, what God is saying. And more and more I'm discovering how true that all really is.

But sometimes, we MUST speak up. Sometimes, silence really is consent. Sometimes, we have no choice by to respond to peoples' lonely cries for help!

And there is only one way to do that. When confronting the kinds of "principalities and powers" referenced in the Letter to the Ephesians, there is only one weapon at our disposal. And it's love! That is our most powerful witness.

It's why so many of the saints of the modern era – people like Martin Luther King Jr., Nelson Mandela, and even pastors and authors like Brian McLaren – these saints often speak about God's people as the Beloved Community. For at the heart of who we are is love! And sometimes that love is the only weapon that can conquer the kinds of sins that have become so powerfully and painfully visible in recent months.

We need to allow the words of these saints to be written on our hearts, just like Scripture. King said that "just as darkness cannot drive out darkness, hate cannot drive out hate. Only love can do that." Mandella told us that "no one is born hating another person. People learn to hate. And if they can learn to hate, so can they learn to love." And Brian McLaren has been encouraging the church for years now to become above all else, a "school of love!"

Church, could it be that the Beatles were right? All we need, is love!

If so, then who are you being called to love? Is it the woman who cuts in front of you at Starbucks, the family member who just loves Donald Trump, the White Supremacist who is filled with more hate than you ever thought could possibly fit into one person's heart, that neighbor who never has anything kind to say about anything? Who are you being called to love; and how can we better do it?

I've decided that people can hate me all they want. They can be angered by my politics, and they can fight, and resist, and disagree with me on everything they want. They can reject me, and my family, and my ideas, and my teachings; and they can get all worked up with the positions I take on all kinds of things. But I am never going to stop loving them. Like burning coals over their heads I am going to strive to love them as God loves them, and trust that that is the greatest and best witness that I can offer them, and the world. I'm going to drive them crazy with my love! Because in the end . . . that love . . . is all that really matters. And we have it. So let's share it. And in so doing, let's change this world . . . all for the glory of God, Amen!

Part 2:

The Summer of 2018

Reclaiming Jesus: Belief #1
June 10, 2018

As the first year of the Trump presidency came to end, people of faith across the country began to realize that the Church needed to take a more formal stance against the ungodliness that was being witnessed on the evening news every single day! Thus Christian leaders came together and prepared "Reclaiming Jesus: A Confession of Faith in a Time of Crisis" and the following sermons explore the six central proclamations of the creed. The introduction to the creed states "we are living through perilous and polarizing times as a nation, with a dangerous crisis of moral and political leadership at the highest levels of our government and in our churches. **We believe the soul of the nation and the integrity of faith are now at stake.**" (Note: the 'bold' is theirs, not mine!)

The faith community was still having trouble 'getting over' the election of Donald Trump; and not because our candidate lost an election, but because the country that we all love was moving toward "false doctrines and political idolatries." And so with humility and prayer, brave Church leaders sought to call the Church to a time of lament, confession, and repentance; that we might return to the Christ we call Lord.

Psalm 138 (CEB)
I give thanks to you with all my heart, LORD.
*   I sing your praise before all other gods.*
I bow toward your holy temple and thank your name
*   for your loyal love and faithfulness*
*   because you have made your name and word*
*   greater than everything else.*
On the day I cried out, you answered me.
*   You encouraged me with inner strength.*
Let all the earth's rulers give thanks to you, LORD,
*   when they hear what you say.*
Let them sing about the LORD's ways
*   because the LORD's glory is so great!*

Even though the LORD is high, he can still see the lowly,
  but God keeps his distance from the arrogant.
Whenever I am in deep trouble, you make me live again;
  you send your power against my enemies' wrath;
  you save me with your strong hand.
The LORD will do all this for my sake. Your faithful love lasts forever,
LORD!
  Don't let go of what your hands have made.

Mark 3:20-35 (CEB)

Jesus entered a house. A crowd gathered again so that it was impossible for him and his followers even to eat. When his family heard what was happening, they came to take control of him. They were saying, "He's out of his mind!"
The legal experts came down from Jerusalem. Over and over they charged, "He's possessed by Beelzebul. He throws out demons with the authority of the ruler of demons."

When Jesus called them together, he spoke to them in a parable: "How can Satan throw Satan out? A kingdom involved in civil war will collapse. And a house torn apart by divisions will collapse. If Satan rebels against himself and is divided, then he can't endure. He's done for. No one gets into the house of a strong person and steals anything without first tying up the strong person. Only then can the house be burglarized. I assure you that human beings will be forgiven for everything, for all sins and insults of every kind. But whoever insults the Holy Spirit will never be forgiven. That person is guilty of a sin with consequences that last forever." He said this because the legal experts were saying, "He's possessed by an evil spirit."

His mother and brothers arrived. They stood outside and sent word to him, calling for him. A crowd was seated around him, and those sent to him said, "Look, your mother, brothers, and sisters are outside looking for you."

He replied, "Who is my mother? Who are my brothers?" Looking around at those seated around him in a circle, he said, "Look, here are my mother and my brothers. Whoever does God's will is my brother, sister, and mother."

Where do I begin with a passage like this? Should we look at the multitudes that followed Jesus, or the radical nature of the message he proclaimed? Should we look at the consequences of a 'house divided'; or a community that doesn't quite grasp the difference between unity and uniformity? Should we consider why Jesus' family was continually trying to rein him in, or why they were so fearful of the implications of his teachings?

This week's lectionary readings, being studied by churches everywhere this morning, are packed with several concepts and ideas worthy of a sermon or two. But in light of all that is going in our nation, and really our world today, I want to jump to the end of the passage and look at Jesus' statement that anyone who does God's will, is part of God's family! And I'd like us to consider that verse from the perspective of Psalmist promising that one day all the rulers of the earth will be united in giving thanks to God, realizing how good and great God really is. I want to do this in the hope that once again we all might discover the unity that comes about when we seek the will of God: whenever we are about the work of the Holy! And I'm not just talking us experiencing that unity here at MVPC; or even about that unity being discovered in the Presbyterian Church, as a whole. Rather, I'm talking about a unity within all of Christendom, and how we might find it.

The Gospel reading says that anyone who does the will of God is Jesus' brother, sister, mother. But what does that really mean?

Well I have come to believe that the answer to that question can be found in a brand-new statement of faith for the Christian Church in America. It's titled "Reclaiming Jesus: A Confession of Faith in a Time of Crisis"; and so beginning this morning, and for the next several weeks, we're going to look at some of the creedal statements that the authors believe can and should unite Christians of every flavor and stripe.

The document was created and signed by some of the most faithful Church leaders in our nation: Black, White, female, male, mainline, independent, evangelical and progressive. Acknowledging one another as family, they all came together around a commitment to reclaim the teachings of Jesus: people you may know; : like Old Testament Scholar from Columbia Presbyterian Seminary, Walter Bruggeman; long-time evangelical author and speaker Tony Campolo; and presiding Bishop of the Episcopal Church and preacher at last month's royal wedding Michael Curry; and also people you may not know but need to know, like: Dr. JoAnne Lyon, General Superintendent of the Wesleyan Church; Ron Sider, Director of Evangelicals for Social Action; and Otis Moss and Barbara Williams-Skinner, co-conveners of the National African-American Clergy Network.

What these people, from all kinds of distinct and diverse Christian faith traditions have affirmed is that today, because of the attempts by so many to exalt political gain above Christian teaching, the Church's identity in Jesus Christ must be lifted up as first and foremost in our lives. These saints have sought to remind us that as the Church of Jesus Christ, we are HIS followers, before we are followers of anyone or anything else. And when particular political platforms undermine our theology, or when the teachings of certain segments of the Church stray from a consistent Biblical or Gospel ethic, we MUST speak up. We must boldly and unapologetically take a stand to reclaim our faith, and to move things back in alignment with the teachings of Jesus. Because just in case we've forgotten this, neither . . . yes neither . . . of America's political parties has the corner on the market of Biblical or theological faithfulness. We all know that, right? Biblical, or theological faithfulness to Jesus Christ is not the goal of either party. That's OUR goal, not theirs! Biblical and theological faithfulness? . . . that's OUR job! And so this sermon is not about Republicans, or Democrats. It's about us, the Church!

The crisis of moral and ethical leadership in our country is OUR problem, and WE are the ones who need to be leading the resistance. We are the ones who need to be speaking truth to power, because the harm that is being inflicted upon our nation, and the world, runs the risk of doing irreparable damage.

So to this end, this new confession of faith lifts up six affirmations, that when understood to be foundational to our life together, have the capacity to unite us in the family of God, and to move us toward God's will for creation. And the first affirmation is this:

"We believe each human being is made in God's image and likeness; and racial bigotry is a brutal denial of the image of God is some of the children of God. Therefore, we reject the resurgence of White supremacy and racism in our nation . . . we commit ourselves to help dismantle the systems and structures that perpetuate White preference and advantage . . . (And) any doctrines or political strategies that use racist resentments, fear, or language must be named as public sin."

Now as I've said before, one would think that this issue would have been resolved by now. I mean the American war against slavery ended 150 years ago; and righteousness won that war! We learned way back then that a house divided cannot stand. And the house that I'm referring to is not America, as much as I would like that to be so! The house that Scripture is referring to in this morning's passage is the Church. It's Christ's Body in the world. And so while the Civil War was an attempt to bring some unity to the American house, the Bible really isn't so much interested in national unity, as it is in Christian unity. God's desire always has been, and always will be, that the Church be united against the enslavement of others. And this is particularly true of the American Church. This notion that America, or Israel, or any other earthy nation can, or even should, be God's beacon of light to the world – that is not a New Testament concept. If the world needs a beacon, that is the job of the Church – the faith community! WE are called to be light to the nations! A nation can't be that light because nations have too many other competing objectives that prevent it from being Light. So as much as we might like to think that America is some kind of chosen city, set on a hill for all the world to admire – that will never be. WE are the city! WE are the ones called to let our light shine. WE – the Church! And friends whenever the Church is tempted to get into bed with the state, we need to remember that WE, the Church, will always be the ones who to eventually suffer. We will be the ones who will be compromised.

So today, in light of where this nation is, the Church's first and perhaps most important affirmation is that each and every one of us is made in God's image and likeness. Racial bigotry is a brutal denial of that reality and there's really nothing debatable about that. We must be united in affirming that White supremacy, preference, and advantage; and all the other markers of the systemic and structural racism that plague our nation today is nothing less than public and corporate sin. It needs to be named and confessed, and then we need to take the lead seeking reconciliation required: whatever that looks like.

And we have to be in agreement on this. That's why you're hearing so much about it here at MVPC. It's why our Justice Small Group is spending so much time reading about it. It's why last year's "Community Conversations" tried to get us talking about it. It's why a small group of us is going to see "The Scottsboro Boys" this afternoon at the Signature Theater. And it's why our congregation is committed to doing a better job of developing relationships with some of the Black congregations in the area.

We need to be setting the example; and once we do, we need to attempt to move out into the rest of society. Because while nations cannot BE Christian, they certainly CAN embrace traits, and practices, and values, that are either more or less reflective of Gospel values. And while nations will never BE the light, they can strive to reflect it. That's what prompted Martin Luther King Jr to say that the Church is called to be "the conscience of the state." Our goal is NOT to become one WITH the state – that is impossible! That's not where we find our unity. Rather, we are to be the state's, or the nation's, conscience. We are the ones who need to be holding nations accountable, by setting an example, and by bringing the way of Jesus to the world.

We, you and me, are the ones called to hold our nation's feet to the fire, that our leaders would always recognize the image of God in everyone. We, you and me, need to be boldly proclaiming that the wonderful diversity of human skin color is nothing more than that, different human skin color! It in no way determines one's value or worth; and certainly does not ever lead to second class status for any of our citizens. The dance that we do together – Black, Brown, Yellow, Red, White – is what creates the glorious rainbow that is God. The whole idea of a 'melting pot' really does help us to enflesh the New Testament concept of family.

And Church, we have to honest with ourselves and confess that we've not always done a very good job of living this out. Oh we've talked about it. Since our founding almost 250 years ago we have talked about equality, about liberty and justice for all. But that didn't apply to people with Black skin; and considering the way America's native people were treated, it certainly didn't apply to people with red skin either!

So this is why I, and so many in the Church today, will not, and cannot, stop talking about the colorism that continues to tear apart our society. It must be addressed, and any person or party that is unwilling to deal with the implicit bias – our unconscious attribution of particular qualities or stereotypes to certain groups of people, simply because they are part of that group – anyone unwilling to deal with that kind of implicit bias must be held accountable. For there is no better example of corporate and societal sin than that.

Jesus' life and ministry were all about valuing everyone, particularly people on the margins . . . those whom society had relegated to the sidelines: sinners, and tax-collectors, prostitutes, and Gentiles, even women, which is where we'll be headed next week. Jesus was able to see the Spirit of God in everyone, and so he valued everyone! There were no second-class citizens in Jesus world, so one has to ask why are there second-class citizens in ours?

I know that many people today are tired of hearing about issues involving race. But as this new confession reveals, it is one of the most important issues facing our Church and our nation today. And while progress continues to be made, we still have a long way to go. There is not a level playing field in our country and so we must address the prejudice, the White supremacy and privilege, and all the other issues that are so systemically evil. And it begins by turning inward and dealing with the implicit bias of our own hearts.

Jim Wallis, President and Founder of Sojourners, who played an important role in the formation of this creed, has said that . . . "the soul of the nation, and the integrity of our faith are at stake." Richard Rohr, Direction of the Center for Action and Contemplation, who also had a hand in the writing, said in a devotional this past week that "God's image within each of us is inherent and irrevocable." And on this there can be no division.

We need to learn to be allies to our siblings of color; and our hearts need to be breaking over all that is breaking their hearts.

When their sons' lives are prematurely cut short by overly aggressive policing, and when their daughters' lives find their way into the pipeline from school to prison: we need to be the ones who stand up and say, "No more!" When racists are not called out and named for who and what they are, and when Brown people are labeled murders and rapists: WE need to be the ones who stand up and say, "No more!" And when seeking to voice their concerns leads these family members to take a stand, or a knee for that matter; WE dare not condemn their frustration with the injustice they're experiencing, but instead we need to understand it, support it, and help explain it!

The Christian house will never know uniformity. We, in this church, will never be one on every political issue that faces our nation. But we CAN know unity around the ways of Christ. And one of the first steps toward that unity involves our "reclaiming Jesus"; and no longer being divided over the image of God existing in all people. We are all part of God's family; and that is the Light in which we all need to be marching.

So let's march together this morning, and as we do, let's sing, and dance, and pray, all in the light of our God.

> We are marching in the light of God;
> > we are marching in the light of God.
> We are marching in the light of God;
> > we are marching in the light of God.
> We are marching, we are marching oho,
> > we are marching in the light of God.
> We are marching, we are marching oho,
> > we are marching in the light of God.

Reclaiming Jesus: Belief #2
June 17, 2018

Psalm 20 (CEB)

I pray that the LORD answers you whenever you are in trouble.
Let the name of Jacob's God protect you.
Let God send help to you from the sanctuary and support you from Zion.
Let God recall your many grain offerings;
let him savor your entirely burned offerings.
Let God grant what is in your heart and fulfill all your plans.
Then we will rejoice that you've been helped.
We will fly our flags in the name of our God.
Let the LORD fulfill all your requests!
Now I know that the LORD saves his anointed one;
God answers his anointed one from his heavenly sanctuary,
answering with mighty acts of salvation achieved by his strong hand.
Some people trust in chariots, others in horses; but we praise the LORD's name.
They will collapse and fall, but we will stand up straight and strong.
9 LORD, save the king! Let him answer us when we cry out!

Galatians 3:23-29 (CEB)

Before faith came, we were guarded under the Law, locked up until faith that was coming would be revealed, so that the Law became our custodian until Christ so that we might be made righteous by faith. But now that faith has come, we are no longer under a custodian. You are all God's children through faith in Christ Jesus. All of you who were baptized into Christ have clothed yourselves with Christ. There is neither Jew nor Greek; there is neither slave nor free; nor is there male and female, for you are all one in Christ Jesus. Now if you belong to Christ, then indeed you are Abraham's descendants, heirs according to the promise.

This morning we are continuing our study of a recent statement of Christian belief, born in the hearts and minds of an extremely diverse group of American Church leaders. In light of all that is going in our country today, these authors have called Christians to: "humbly reconsider what it means to proclaim that Jesus, and no one else, is Lord!" The statement is titled

"Reclaiming Jesus: A Confession of Faith in a Time of Crisis", and it is a declaration of what it means to be 'in Christ,' as stated in the passage that I just read from Galatians. More than just bunch of words on a piece of paper, to be read now and then and subsequently filed away somewhere, it is a creedal statement intended to truly shape the way we live our lives, in "such a time as this!"

Several weeks ago I attended a gathering of clergy where this confession was presented, and Tony Campolo, one of the authors, offered a short homily. In talking about the unity of the Church that he hoped a confession like this might help to foster, he said "most of us want it, and some of us even strive for it, but there are simply too many church teachings that continue to make it extremely difficult. Just look at Holy Communion, he said. "You've got the Roman Catholics at one end of the spectrum who want the bread to turn into the body. And then you've got Baptists like me at the other end wanting the wine to turn into juice."

I'll give you a second on that one, because it really is kinda' funny!

Jesus unites. His way makes us one! But doctrine? Doctrine divides! Church law sets us in different Church camps!

Again this week, unity, is what the Scripture passage for the day is calling us toward; and as far as this confession of faith is concerned, unity can only be found in a faith that rejects any and every form of oppression. Belief number one, which we looked at last week, declared that the image and likeness of God exists in all people, and therefore racial bigotry of any sort is a denial of this theological truth and nothing less than public sin. That's where we were last week. This week, we're considering belief #2, which makes this affirmation: "We believe that we are one body in Christ, and therefore there is to be no oppression based upon race, gender, identity, or class."

No oppression based upon race, gender, identity, or class!

Now since we dealt with race last week; and since we looked at some of the issues surrounding gender several months ago, and will also be dealing with gender issues in additional settings this fall, this morning my focus is going to be on that term 'identity' – which is a reference to sexual identity. Today, in the middle of what has become known "Pride Month", we're going to tackle the subject which, after abortion, may be one of the most divisive issues facing some churches today: and that is the treatment of our LGBTQ brothers and sisters.

Now interestingly, society at large has been far more receptive to the Spirit's movement in this area than we in the Church have: which I must say is a sad statement on the state of the faith community in our country. Perhaps without even knowing it, society has followed the Spirit's lead: knowing full well that this is a justice issue, and that discrimination on the basis of one's sexual orientation is simply unacceptable. But we in the Church? We in the Church, and in far too many faith communities, have been slow to come to this realization. Sadly, there are still far too many people of all faiths who refuse to embrace anything but the heterosexual lifestyle. And they see it as their job to hold society back from what is perceived to be a slow and steady descent toward immorality.

Never the less, I, and a growing chorus of Biblical Scholars, theologians, and average Christ-followers just like many of you: we believe that as the Spirit continues to shed more light on this issue, the Church and the world must recognize that, as the saying goes . . . God is less concerned with WHO a person loves, and more concerned with THAT a person loves. And so when it comes to the many LGBTQ issues facing us today, the faith community needs to be far more supportive than we have been and not IN SPITE of our faith, but BECAUSE of our faith.

In his book "God vs. Gay", author Jay Michaelson points out that a close reading of both the Hebrew Bible and the Greek New Testament, along with the latest data on the science of sexual orientation, all reveal that diversity in all its forms, including sexual diversity, is part of the beauty of creation. And this realization need not threaten us!

Scripture actually has nothing at all to say about committed, same-gender relationships; and when it comes to ordination in the

Church, homosexuality is as irrelevant as one's right-handed or left-handedness! Are there passages that condemn sexual exploitation, as well as hetero or homosexual promiscuity? Most definitely! But Jesus says nothing about homosexuality . . . absolutely nothing. And it's not like it was uncommon in his day. He certainly would have been familiar with it, and yet nowhere does he condemn it, or for that matter even address it. This is what has led so many of us to believe that it was simply a non-issue for him.

The hesitancy of many in the Church to rid themselves of their homophobia, and so many of the prejudices that come along with it, are really NOT born in any kind of sound theology. Rather, I would contend, such thinking finds its roots in a form of Christian dualism that has had a strangle-hold on the Church for generations: a dualism that promotes an us-vs-them perspective on humanity; a your-either-in-or-your-out way of thinking about God's love and grace. In reality, the kind of resistance seen in many segments of the Church today is all about our constant and continual "othering." We meet people who are not like us: people who look, live, or love differently than we do, and we "other" them! We treat them as if they are less, simply because they are different.

No, Blacks are not like Whites. Women are not like men. The poor are not like the rich. Homosexuals are not like heterosexuals. We are indeed all different. But when our 'othering' divides people into categories of what is acceptable and what is not, marking certain groups of people as being less than others . . . less than they are in the eyes of God . . . well friends, that too, is nothing less than sin, personal and public!

That's what is actually being shared with the Church at Galatia in this morning's Scripture passage. The author is telling them, and us, that in the Body, no one is superior to anyone else. Jews aren't better than Gentiles. Men aren't more valuable than women. Slaves aren't inferior to their masters. We are who we are – and none of it matters to God. And particularly today, we in the Church must remain united around this belief, regardless of what is going on in the world around us.

Sadly we've not always done this. The Church has been telling women for centuries, and in some instances is still sending the same message today, that they are the weaker sex. We've subtly, and not so subtly, told men that we are to have authority over women, leading us to wrongly believe that we can do whatever we want, whenever we want, however we want. But if the 'me too' movement has shown us anything, it has pulled the curtain back on the consequences of such oppression.

Now this is not the only time that we in the Church have not been on the right side of history. We've used the Bible to justify the institution of slavery, and current forms of racism. We've used it to account for the health and wealth of certain segments of society, as well as the poverty of other segments. Now today, we are seeing people try to use the Bible to justify the separating of women and children crossing our southern boarder for asylum – which we'll be dealing with in greater detail next week . . . amateur Bible scholars and religious people all using our faith to rally their political base, for causes and agendas that are simply not in the least bit reflective of Jesus' teachings. And when it comes to sexuality, here again we've used Scripture to oppress countless women and men, who were likely already struggling with their identity, and added fuel to the fires of their self-hatred.

The suicides of Kate Spade and Anthony Bourdain two weeks ago have brought to all of our attention the growing mental health epidemic that suicide is becoming in this country; but it's especially problematic among our youth. It is the second leading cause of death among young people between the ages of 10 and 24 today; and gay and lesbian youth? They contemplate suicide at 3x the rate of heterosexual youth, and they are 5x times more likely to actually attempt suicide. And while things are indeed changing, coming out and admitting first to yourself, and then to others, that you are gay, lesbian, or trans – well the people I've encountered in my ministry have taught me that we in the straight, cisgender community will never be able to fathom how difficult that really is. And it only becomes more complicated as we learn more and more about the gender and sexuality continuum.

The acceptance of homosexuality is also very difficult for so many because the world's shift in thinking has happened so fast! The confusion, and even fear, are understandable. But confusion and fear can never be used to justify behavior that shuns or condemns people simply because of who they love.

If by chance anyone listening to this sermon, either here this morning, or on-line at some point in the future, or if you are reading these words in a book, and struggling with your sexual identity, please know that you are deeply and dearly loved . . . every part of who you . . . every part of who you were created to be. And you need to know that doesn't EXclude the sexual expression that best suits you. It INcludes it. You're not loved by God in spite of your sexuality. God loves that about you just as much as God loves the texture of your hair, the passions of your heart, and the warmth of your smile. And you can never, ever let anyone, ever, lead you to believe differently!

This is the message the Church is called to proclaim, and today as much as ever! You see today, Churches and other radical religious groups, as well as other fringe segments of our population, continue to threaten all of us by threatening our LGBTQ siblings. This past week was the second anniversary of the Pulse Club shooting in Florida and we need to remember the hate that was behind that tragedy! Those who carry such hate, and inflict it upon others; those who don't have to deal with, or interact with, or who worse yet want discriminate again those they believe are living in a manner that is inconsistent with their views of God, marriage, love, or sexual expression – friends those people and positions need to be challenged regardless of how significantly those beliefs are embedded in their faith. Because faith is never an excuse for prejudice! Please hear that. Freedom of religion does not give any of us the right to discriminate against another person for the lives they chose to live. Ever!

Here in America we have the right to believe whatever we want to believe, and to practice whatever faith we choose to practice . . . UNTIL that faith oppresses or infringes upon the rights of others. That friends, is not the way of Jesus, nor can it ever be masqueraded as the will of God.

What is so interesting to me is that the only people Jesus ever really challenged in the Gospels were the religious people – those who thought their laws needed to be forced upon everyone else. The Pharisees and Sadducees were the people for whom Jesus had the harshest words. Which should tell us that any attitude or behavior of ours, that in any way oppress others, on the basis of their sexual identity, their gender, or countless other unimportant labels that we're so prone to want to force upon them – that all needs to be challenged and dismissed. For there are no second class of citizens within the Body of Christ.

Qu'ils mangent de la brioche.

Do you know that phrase? It's the infamous and condescending phrase, that means "Let them eat cake". Thought by many to have to have been spoken by Marie Antoinette in the 18th century upon learning that the French peasants had no bread; there is actually no evidence she ever said such a thing. In fact, Marie Antoinette was known as someone who had great sympathy for the poor. Nevertheless old legends die hard, and so it is hard to change the belief that she had an overt insensitivity to those on the margins of French society.

Sadly, today, there are far too many people in the Church of Jesus Christ who have an overt insensitivity toward others. Far too many who are continually trying to push more and more people to the margins of our society: the immigrant and refugee, the poor and underemployed, women, sometimes even old white men, as well as the LGBTQ community. We so 'other' them, that we don't even notice them. And if we do, the unconscious and implicit bias that I talked about last week, perverts the way we see them.

But this simply cannot be the case for those of us who claim to be part of the Church of Jesus Christ. Here, we all ate cake! We, more than anyone, need to be embrace the idea that in Jesus, we are one: all of us! And no matter what label another person wears, we cannot, and should not, separate ourselves from them. They all need to be welcome here, truly, everyone . . . gay, straight, trans, bi, rich, poor, young, old, single, married, divorced, and on and on and on.

We, as a portion of Christendom, known as Mount Vernon Presbyterian . . . we need to be sure that all people, everywhere, know that in name of Jesus, our doors, and hearts, will always be open. Our behavior, our attitudes, our hospitality – it will all be determined and shaped, not by the supreme court, but by the living Word, Jesus. And so we here, we will eat cake with everyone, and we will bake cakes for everyone. Because here, all are welcome!

(NOTE: This sermon was preached after the Supreme Court of the United States ruled in favor of a Colorado baker who refused to bake a cake to celebrate the marriage of a gay couple because of a religious objection. Thus, the 'let them eat cake' illustration! At the end of worship, during the postlude, our ushers carried large tables into our worship space with pieces of cake for everyone to enjoy! It was a very 'sweet' Sunday!)

Reclaiming Jesus: Belief #3

June 24, 2018

Psalm 9:9-20 (CEB)
The LORD is a safe place for the oppressed—a safe place in difficult times.
Those who know your name trust you because you have not abandoned any who
seek you, LORD.
Sing praises to the LORD, who lives in Zion!
    Proclaim his mighty acts among all people!
Because the one who avenges bloodshed remembers those who suffer;
    the LORD hasn't forgotten their cries for help.
Have mercy on me, LORD! Just look how I suffer because of those who hate
me.
But you are the one who brings me back from the very gates of death
    so I can declare all your praises, so I can rejoice in your salvation in the gates
of
    Daughter Zion.
The nations have fallen into the hole they themselves made! Their feet are
caught
    in the very net they themselves hid!
The LORD is famous for the justice he has done; it's his own doing that the
wicked
    are trapped.
Let the wicked go straight to the grave,
    the same for every nation that forgets God.
Because the poor won't be forgotten forever,
    the hope of those who suffer won't be lost for all time.
Get up, LORD! Don't let people prevail! Let the nations be judged before you.
Strike them with fear, LORD. Let the nations know they are only human.

Matthew 25:31-45 (CEB)
"Now when the Human One comes in his majesty and all his angels are with
him, he will sit on his majestic throne. All the nations will be gathered in front
of him. He will separate them from each other, just as a shepherd separates the
sheep from the goats. He will put the sheep on his right side. But the goats he
will put on his left.

"Then the king will say to those on his right, 'Come, you who will receive good
things from my Father. Inherit the kingdom that was prepared for you before

the world began. I was hungry and you gave me food to eat. I was thirsty and you gave me a drink. I was a stranger and you welcomed me. I was naked and you gave me clothes to wear. I was sick and you took care of me. I was in prison and you visited me.'

"Then those who are righteous will reply to him, 'Lord, when did we see you hungry and feed you, or thirsty and give you a drink? When did we see you as a stranger and welcome you, or naked and give you clothes to wear? When did we see you sick or in prison and visit you?'

"Then the king will reply to them, 'I assure you that when you have done it for one of the least of these brothers and sisters of mine, you have done it for me.'
"Then he will say to those on his left, 'Get away from me, you who will receive terrible things. Go into the unending fire that has been prepared for the devil and his angels. I was hungry and you didn't give me food to eat. I was thirsty and you didn't give me anything to drink. I was a stranger and you didn't welcome me. I was naked and you didn't give me clothes to wear. I was sick and in prison, and you didn't visit me.'

"Then they will reply, 'Lord, when did we see you hungry or thirsty or a stranger or naked or sick or in prison and didn't do anything to help you?' Then he will answer, 'I assure you that when you haven't done it for one of the least of these, you haven't done it for me.'

Reclaiming Jesus: A Confession of Faith in a time of Crisis" has six affirmation for the Church today. This morning we're looking at affirmation number 3, which reads as follows:

We believe how we treat the hungry, the thirsty, the naked, the stranger, the sick, and the prisoner is how we treat Christ himself. God calls us to protect and seek justice for those who are poor and vulnerable, and our treatment of people who are "oppressed," "strangers," "outsiders," or otherwise considered "marginal", is a test of our relationship to God.

Therefore we reject . . . language and policies (that) debase and abandon the most vulnerable children of God. We strongly deplore the growing attacks on immigrants and refugees, who are being made into cultural and political targets; and we . . . remind our churches that (according to Leviticus 19) God makes the treatment of the "strangers" among us a test of faith . . . (So) we commit ourselves to . . . finding solutions that reflect the wisdom of people from different political parties and philosophies to seek the common good; (for) protecting the poor is a central commitment of Christian discipleship.

That affirmation, along with this morning's Gospel lesson, both remind us that what we do to others, we do to Jesus. They're in agreement: the way we treat the immigrant, the foreigner, and the refugee is a signpost of our faith. And I'm not sure any creedal statement or Scripture passage could be any more relevant to these days in which we are living.

There are a variety of issues that divide the Church: always have been and always will be. We embrace different opinions on everything from abortion rights to gun control, from the meaning of the sacraments to the efficacy of prayer. But when it comes to the issue before us this morning, the treatment of immigrants and aliens in a foreign land, there is simply no wiggle room. Our faith is very clear.

Exodus tells us – "you shall not oppress an immigrant." Leviticus says – "the immigrant who resides with you shall be to you as the citizen among you." In Deuteronomy we read – "cursed be anyone who deprives the immigrant of justice"; and in Jeremiah – "do no wrong or violence to the immigrant." So put these passages of Scripture alongside of Jesus' own experiences both AS an immigrant and WITH immigrants, together with this morning's passage from Matthew and the 92 other times where Jesus tells us to love our neighbor, and it becomes very clear that there is only one way to understand our faith's teachings about the treatment of immigrants.

Is it any wonder that so many faith communities here in America and around the world have been outraged by all that has been going on among our southern border in recent weeks? And if taking children away from their parents is not enough to offend our sense of discipleship and basic human decency, then surely using the Bible to try and justify such action, should. The proof texting that has been attempted by some – using portions of Scripture that were used by the Church 200 years ago to justify slavery, and 75 years ago as a means to encourage the support of Nazism – such Biblical malpractice is just one more reason why so many are walking away from the institutional church today. People know that holy words, read and applied in a manner that lead to actions which deny or betray the love, grace, and mercy of God, must always be rejected.

That's what we've been considering for the past three weeks now. Whether talking about the way we treat our siblings of color, women, the LGBTQ community, or immigrants and foreigners among us – prejudice of any sort is nothing less than a denial of the Christian faith and a form of public sin. And ironically, some of the most religiously or theologically uninformed among us, seem to have recognized this long before way too many people of faith!

When will we realize that when Christ followers are forced to choose between the laws of God and the laws of the state, the choice should always be an easy one? We are always citizens of God's 'kin'dom first, and that citizenship comes before any other national allegiance. And I sometimes wonder if we get that? In our professing that Jesus is Lord we are declaring that we follow him before any other worldly ruler. And it is absurd that so many of us still don't get this; or worse yet, that perhaps we do, but we allow our politics to poison our judgement – confusing the way and will of God with the party or the platform of our politician of choice.

Like the racial bigotry that we looked at two weeks ago, and the homophobia that we considered last week, Church, this is not a partisan issue. Separating fathers and mothers from their children is simply not acceptable, no matter how much of a deterrent some might think such heinous actions to be. The Bible, our faith tradition, and the ways of Jesus, simply do not give us that kind of an option.

Perhaps, like some of you, I would love a Scripture that put some parameters on the way we're supposed to treat the stranger and alien among us. But it doesn't! As with most issues related to our caring for the least among us, God doesn't offer any qualifiers.

Jesus never says, "Feed the hungry, unless . . . they're lazy." He never says, "Clothe the naked, unless . . . they won't stop having kids that they can't really afford to care for." He never says, "care for the immigrant, and the refugee, unless . . . they cross your borders illegally." No! As hard as it makes things, Jesus doesn't let us off the hook that way . . . ever!

So this morning, creeds and Scripture are both calling US to take the lead when it comes to all that is going on in our country today. And by 'us', please know I'm not talking about one particular party over and above the other. When I talk about US, I'm talking about the faith community. I'm talking about the Church! THIS church! Because neither the Republicans NOR the Democrats have displayed an ability to get anything done on this issue. That too is what we've seen over the past couple of weeks. That's why the Church is finally speaking out the way it is.

Last week alone, the Stated Clerk of our denomination issued a statement reminding us of Jesus' command to care for the foreigner. The United Methodist Church came out with a similar statement. Several local Presbyterian sessions also took a stand as well . . . because there are some things about which the Church simply cannot remain silent. The way we treat one another – the way we treat families, and especially children, the most vulnerable among us – is the way we treat Jesus! And when a government fails to exhibit God's grace, mercy, and love, then the Church, as the moral conscience of the State, must speak out. For we, are citizens of God's kindom, and Jesus alone, is our Lord!

The implicit bias that we looked at two weeks ago, and the othering that I talked about last week – we need to confess that is has led far too many of us to believe that immigrants are bad people, crossing our borders illegally, and coming from Radical Muslim countries. We're told again and again that they are doing nothing but killing and raping Americans. But that is simply not the case – not when it comes to the overwhelming majority of immigrants in this country. And friends, these facts, these truths, and others like them, need to be shaping our Christian response to all that is going on today. For when we learn the facts and let go of all the political propaganda that is being shoved in our faces today, I have no doubt that that our response will be become more humane, more compassionate, and more consistent with the way of Jesus.

And that's really the point isn't it? No one wants to abandon laws. But even laws need to be enforced in ways that respect a person's humanity! None of us, ever, have the right to treat anyone, with anything less than love and grace and mercy that we'd show Jesus. That's the whole point of this morning's passage. We need to be treating everyone with dignity and respect. Because the way we treat one another, is the way we are treating Jesus. This morning's passage is NOT about OUR separating the sheep from the goats, even though that we love to do that, right? Don't we love to separate people, into different camps . . . the good ones and the bad ones; the ones we like and the ones we don't like; the ones with whom we agree and the ones with whom we don't agree. We love doing that – separating and dividing people in a way that allows us to determine who are sheep, and who are goats.

But that is not the point of the passage. Jesus is NOT telling this story because he wants US to start doing the separating. He is telling the story because he wants us to understand that all of us, both sheep and goats, will be judged by how we treat others. And not just those we like, or those we agree with, but everyone. However we are understanding judgement, goodness and Godliness are determined by how we treat everyone, especially the least among us!

Do you remember the movie "The Green Mile" from way back in 1999? It starred Tom Hanks as a death row corrections officer, and Michael Clarke Duncan, a physically imposing but mentally challenged, Black man, wrongly accused of raping two white girls. Now because Tom Hanks cannot possibly play a character who is anything less than kind and compassionate, his treatment of this prisoner on death row, reminds us all of what it means to show justice with mercy, and to display love and grace even to the least among us.

In one of their final conversations, the wrongly convicted mane says that he's ready to die. He just wants it all to be over. He's tired of people being so ugly to each other. He's tired of all the pain in the world. There's just too much of it all, and it's suffocating him!

Church, I don't know about you, but the ugliness I'm seeing in our country these days, seems to be everywhere, and it's suffocating me! And my fear is that we're starting to use the ugliness we see in others' attitudes and behavior, to justify our own. And that can never be!

I try very hard to keep church and state issues separate, but that is extremely difficult these days. Because one of the things that have always made this country so special is that we have sought to stand on the side of good; and that even our laws, have been enforced with grace.

Have we made mistakes, and fallen short? Of course we have; and I will be the first to admit that! But in most instances, we are seeking to acknowledge our deficiencies – not hide or deny them. And when we've recognized them, we've sought, and are still seeking, to correct them. For the most part, our history is one of having tried to stand on the side of goodness, and righteousness. We have tried to value truth and honesty. We have tried to honor integrity and justice.

But that has become extremely hard these days, and if we in the Body of Christ cannot, and do not, stand up; if WE do not resist that trend, together . . . then who will?

So may that be our goal. In spite of the negative examples being set all around us, may we never forget that Jesus alone is our Lord; and that what we do unto the least among us, we do unto him.

Reclaiming Jesus: Belief #4
July 1, 2018

In an age of twisted values we have lost the truth we need.
In sophisticated language we have justified our greed.
By our struggle for possessions we have robbed the poor and weak.
Hear our dry and heal our nation; your forgiveness Lord we seek.

We have built discrimination on our prejudice and fear.
Hatred swiftly turns to cruelty if we hold resentments dear.
For communities divided by the walls of class and race,
Hear our cry and heal our nation; show us Lord, your love and grace.
(In an age of twisted values, vss. 1 & 3)

Psalm 130 (CEB)

I cry out to you from the depths, LORD, MY Lord, listen to my voice!
    Let your ears pay close attention to my request for mercy!
If you kept track of sins, LORD—my Lord, who would stand a chance?
But forgiveness is with you— that's why you are honored.

I hope, LORD. My whole being hopes, and I wait for God's promise.
My whole being waits for my Lord— more than the night watch waits for morning;
    yes, more than the night watch waits for morning!
Israel, wait for the LORD! Because faithful love is with the LORD;
    because great redemption is with our God!
He is the one who will redeem Israel from all its sin.

John 8:31-36 (CEB)

Jesus said to the Jews who believed in him, "You are truly my disciples if you remain faithful to my teaching. Then you will know the truth, and the truth will set you free."

They responded, "We are Abraham's children; we've never been anyone's slaves. How can you say that we will be set free?"

Jesus answered, "I assure you that everyone who sins is a slave to sin. A slave isn't a permanent member of the household, but a child is. Therefore, if the Son makes you free, you really will be free.

My son Jacob has not always been as big as he is today! It wasn't until he started working in his gym in college and working out on a daily basis, that he buffed up. Up until that time he was actually smaller than me: taller, yes! But I could still . . . take him, if you know what I mean. Or at least I thought I could.

I know I could when he was little: up to and perhaps through Middle School. I would wrestle with him and Stefan all the time, usually on the family room floor. And what I remember most about those times was always knowing how to make Jacob "give up." You see Jake has always been claustrophobic, and so all I would have to do back then was just hold him so tight that he couldn't move. I'd actually lay on top of him, and that's all it would take, and he would start screaming and give up. Still today, just wearing a pair of leather, laced, shoes, gets Jacob's feet feeling claustrophobic.

Anyone else like that – you just don't like being constrained? Small, confined spaces are like strait jackets that have the capacity to bring you to the brink of a panic attack.

Well in this morning's Scripture reading from the Gospel of John, we discover that sin is kinda' like that. It's kind of like a strait jacket. In contrast to truth, sin enslaves us, binding our hearts and minds, our souls and spirits, often in ways that we don't even realize. The lies it tells us, cage our very being, and negatively impact everything about us. That's why the 9th commandment is so important for us – not bearing false witness, not lying, or being untruthful – because to live according to that which is simply not true, hurts us and those around us. As people of God we are to honor and respect truth; and not doing so is like putting everyone in a strait jacket.

World renown Biblical scholar Walter Bruggeman, in speaking on our 4th affirmation in "Reclaiming Jesus: A confession of faith in a time of crisis" several weeks ago, said that what this commandment means is that we shall not create fake worlds in which to dwell, simple because it may appear convenient. He said, and I quote, "as long as we dwell in a culture of lies, we will never be the land of the free and the home of the brave, but rather the land of the frightened and the home of the anxious."

This is the creed's fourth affirmation:

> We believe that truth is morally central to our personal and public lives. Jesus promises, "You will know the truth, and the truth will set you free." (John 8:32) Therefore, we reject the practice and pattern of lying that is invading our political and civil life . . . (for its normalization) presents a profound moral danger to the fabric of society."

Now this particular affirmation was obviously included because these days, everyone seems to think that everyone else is lying, about everything under the sun. And while we all might have different ideas about who is or isn't telling the truth, I hope we can all agree that lying is simply not a healthy practice. The Gospel according to John, as well as several other passages throughout our Scripture, make it very clear truthful living, is right living; and that a culture of lies violates that rightness. It is nothing less than sinful; and that is the great concern being lifted up in the 8th chapter of John's Gospel.

The writers of this creedal statement that we've been looking at for the past few weeks are very concerned with the spoken lies that are so freely coming from all segments of our public life today. But it goes deeper than the kinds of lies that children tell, untruths designed to help them get away with something they know to be wrong, untruths told when they don't want to be scolded for doing something, they to be wrong. That kind of lying is "bearing false witness," and it's what the ninth commandment is all about. It *may* very well be a concern today; but this morning's passage, as well as the creedal statement, seek to go much deeper.

The Greek word used in today's passage is *ale'thia*, and it is a word that was used when referencing a deep sense of moral rightness.

That is the truth that the writer of John has Jesus addressing in this morning's passage; and where sinful living puts and keeps us in bondage, right and truthful living bring freedom.

Now for us Presbyterians, settling on what this truth is doesn't need to be as hard as we might think; for our Confessional Statements and our denomination's constitution tell us that there really is only one truth around which we seek to build our lives. And that truth is evident in the most basic question that is asked of anyone joining a PCUSA congregation. Who knows what it is?

Exactly – who is your Lord and Savior? That's the only question our constitution says we need to ask of new and potential members. Who is your Lord and Savior? Because you see, for us, Jesus is our truth! And it is that truth that can, and should, unite us.

We as much as anyone, know that when the ways of Christ govern our lives, we find freedom. And when they don't, when we allow other things to govern the way we live our lives, we are lead to ways that are NOT of God, and they do little more than wrap us up in their sinful claustrophobic tentacles, binding and enslaving us in falsehoods and lies that harm, and kill, and destroy.

Church, unlike the other three affirmations that we've considered over the past few weeks, this concept is so very basic that I can't help but wonder why it's so difficult. You see the truth that sets us free, is that simple truth that Jesus is Lord. It is the simple truth that our lives are to be governed and led by the will and ways of the Christ. And when we seek to live that out, we find freedom.

So what has happened to us? What has happened to our understanding of the way of Jesus? How can there be so much conflict about what that means, or what it looks like? How much further apart can we get from one another? How much more polarized can we become when it comes to something that is really so very simple?

We all know that in some instances, truth is indeed a matter of perspective. And we see this in the political world all the time. Statistics are offered, and statements are made, that are indeed true, but that can sometimes lead us to conclusions that are not! The truth is skewed in ways that lead us and others to untruths.

But is it really that hard for us to put our lives alongside of the life of Jesus, and see where things match up, and where they don't? Is that really all that difficult to do?

If what we're doing is not loving, it is not of God. Period. For God IS love. And that's God's way in the world. That's his way. "The greatest of these is love!" Have we not heard that enough? It's Jesus' way, and it's the only way that is ever going to be able to unite such a polarized world.

I have a Baptist pastor friend from Erie, PA, where I served back in the 1990s, and he recently shared this quote "Earth isn't heaven. So lower your expectations!" He had just visited another pastor that we both knew, and that guy had used that line in his sermon.

And when I read it, I thought . . . what? And so because I am who I am, I had to push back, and challenge him, and remind him that Jesus himself told us to pray that God's will might be done on earth as it is in heaven. I told him that at least for me, as a Presbyterian, I embrace a participatory eschatology – meaning that however one understands heaven, it involves a new earth here, and now. And that new world is one that we, and all people of God, are responsible for bringing into being. We have all been called to partner with all that the Spirit is already doing, to make this notion of heaven on earth a reality. This is part of what it means to say that Jesus is Lord. It's our way of acknowledging that this is God's world, and that we are going to strive to live accordingly; never *lowering* our expectations but *raising* them; always seeking God's greater desires for creation. And any theology that regards faithful living is 'lowering our expectations', and theology that regards salvation as being about little more than escape plan from the brokenness of earth, so that we can get somewhere else, up there, where all of our expectation will finally be met . . . folks, that line of thinking simply lacks any theological integrity.

But so often, this doesn't make sense to us. And it doesn't make sense to us because we in the White, American Church, live lives of privilege, and we really don't need, or want, anything to change here on earth. That is the lie that we have been told for years, and it is the lie that too many continue to tell even today. Because it's far easier for us to make faith into the discipline of simply believing certain things, than it requiring us to actually have to change certain things, or to really seek the transformation and new life that are at the heart of the Gospel.

So the truth that can set us free, has become a lie; and it involves settling for things as they are right now, and waiting until we get to heaven to experience the reign of God revealed in the Bible.

Howard Thurman, a Black man raised in the south, early in the 20th century, who went on to become one of America's finest theologians, talks about Jesus message and ministry being all about the transformation of this world: never lowering our expectations, but always seeking greater obedience and faithfulness, justice and love. Thurman's life was all about siding with and caring for the poor. It was about seeking to lift up all people, but particularly those on the margins, because that's what Jesus did.

Thurman writes in his book "Jesus and the Disinherited" that "Christianity, as it was born in the mind of (Jesus, a) Jewish teacher and thinker, appears as a technique of survival for the oppressed." And what he means is that Jesus knew that the world could change, if people just changed. And that is what our faith should aspire us to seek.

But for we in White America? . . . we have way too much to lose, don't we? Why do things need to change?

You see, since the days of Constantine, the Church has known nothing but power; and that power has sustained us for almost 2000 years, AND, that power has shaped our understanding and teaching of the Gospel. For most of us, life here has been pretty good. So why think that change has anything to do with life on earth? Instead, let's make change and transformation, let's make freedom for the oppressed and sight for blind something that will found in the afterlife.

But Church, Jesus said that the 'kin'dom of God was at hand. He came to give the oppressed hope now, encouraging them towards a more truthful way of living in this life, because he knew that things could actually change! He knew that freedom and peace, justice and joy, and all the other blessings of this life could be shared by all, and not just hoarded by those with power and privilege.

This is the truth that Jesus came to proclaim. But the power that the Church had come to possess, became so attractive and alluring, that we suddenly decided we weren't so sure we really wanted anything to change. And so it was just easier to start talking about truth, and justice, and real love, as the things of heaven, to be discovered not here, but in the afterlife.

This is why the Gospel has become less and less about God's 'kin'dom on earth, and more about earth not being heaven, so . . . let's lower our expectations. It's why so many oppressed communities spend so much time talking about "crossing the Jordan" or "chariots swinging low to carry people home." It wasn't until they began recapturing Jesus' theology of liberation, that salvation became about so much more than going to heaven when we die. Only then did the truth of our faith surface, and people began to realize that the freedom that is at the heart of the Gospel, is the truth that new life is for all people, here, and now! That is the truth that can set us all free. And that is the truth, to which the Reclaiming Jesus creed is calling us.

Now people like my friend in Erie will continue to try and keep us thinking that life here is the best we can do; and that we need to just lower our expectations until we get to heaven. They will continue to preach a privileged Gospel, that allows those in power to remain in power, and those with wealth to keep their wealth; assuring everyone else that the depth of their struggle in this life will one day be matched by the joy and justice of heaven. So just wait and be patient. Wife, being abused by your husband, just wait! Father, burying your young black son, way too soon, be patient! Immigrant, fleeing gang-violence that is threatening your life and the life of your family, just hang in there.

After all, patience is a virtue, right? . . . a gift that we all need to learn to cultivate. Have we forgotten that blessed are the persecuted? Did we forget that suffering produces endurance, and endurance character?

Friends, the truth of the Gospel – the truth that sets us free, and that has the capacity to restore the moral fabric of not just of our nation but of the world, is that Jesus alone is Lord! He alone is our firm foundation, and the only truth worth embracing; and anything and everything that in anyway denies that, is a lie!

This morning's closing hymn is all about twisted values; and when I reflect on the days in which we're living, I'm not sure there is a more relevant hymn in our hymnal. As I indicated last week, our government, made up of leaders we've elected, from both political parties, is failing us. So send thoughts and prayers, resist and protest if that your calling, but most important of all, keep on keepin' on. Live out what many of us believe to be the very first creed of Christianity, that "Jesus is Lord". And do that by seeking truth: by pursuing holy justice, by seeking righteous peace, by exhibiting unrestrained hospitality, and by displaying extravagant love . . . for God's sake, Amen.

Reclaiming Jesus: Belief #5

July 8, 2018

Psalm 48 (CEB)

In the city belonging to our God, the LORD is great and so worthy of praise!
His holy mountain is a beautiful summit, the joy of the whole world.
    Mount Zion, in the far north, is the city of the great king.
God is in its fortifications, revealing himself as a place of safety.

Look: the kings assembled themselves, advancing all together—
    when they saw it, they were stunned; they panicked and ran away frightened.
Trembling took hold of them right there— like a woman giving birth,
    or like the east wind when it smashes the ships of Tarshish.
Just like we had heard, now we've seen it for ourselves
    in the city of the LORD of heavenly forces, in the city of our God.
    May God make it secure forever! Selah
We dwell on your faithful love, God, in your temple.
Your praise, God, just like your reputation, extends to the far corners of the
earth.
    Your strong hand is filled with righteousness.
Let Mount Zion be glad; let the towns of Judah rejoice
    because of your acts of justice!
Walk around Zion; go all the way around it; count its towers.
Examine its defenses closely; tour its fortifications
    so that you may tell future generations:
"This is God, our God, forever and always!
    He is the one who will lead us even to the very end."

Mark 10:35-45

James and John, Zebedee's sons, came to Jesus and said, "Teacher, we want
you to do for us whatever we ask."

"What do you want me to do for you?" he asked.

They said, "Allow one of us to sit on your right and the other on your left when
you enter your glory."

Jesus replied, "You don't know what you're asking! Can you drink the cup I
drink or receive the baptism I receive?"

"We can," they answered.

Jesus said, "You will drink the cup I drink and receive the baptism I receive, but to sit at my right or left hand isn't mine to give. It belongs to those for whom it has been prepared."

Now when the other ten disciples heard about this, they became angry with James and John. Jesus called them over and said, "You know that the ones who are considered the rulers by the Gentiles show off their authority over them and their high-ranking officials order them around. But that's not the way it will be with you. Whoever wants to be great among you will be your servant. Whoever wants to be first among you will be the slave of all, for the Human One didn't come to be served but rather to serve and to give his life to liberate many people."

A re we smoking what we're selling?"

That's how the young pastor tried to get us thinking about whether or not we were practicing what we preach. He was leading one of the sessions at a conference I attended back at Princeton Seminary a few months ago, and still today, when I reflect on what he said I have to laugh.

"Are we smoking what we're selling?"

When he said it, I looked at the friend sitting next to me, smiled, and thought "Wow, things sure have changed . . . even at Princeton Seminary."

Unfortunately, when it comes to his topic – namely, Evangelism – I don't think ANYthing has changed. We Presbyterians still struggle with one of the most basic elements of our faith – sharing it! Which is why we pastors spend so much time preaching about it. We all know that it's important, and that doing so is central to taking the Gospel to the ends of the earth. But actually doing it – living out Jesus' mandate to make disciples of all nations – well, that's another story.

Now if you've actually read the text of "Reclaiming Jesus: A confession of faith in a time of crisis", which we've been studying for the past several weeks now, then you're probably saying to yourself, "Wait a minute Bob, I don't remember seeing anything in there about evangelism."

But I am more and more convinced that is precisely what affirmation number five is all about: "We believe that Christ's way of leadership is servanthood, not domination."

The entire statement is actually a little longer, but this portion sums it all up very nicely; and I'm realizing more and more that really is where evangelism begins . . . with our learning what it means to be a servant.

You see, too many of us think that evangelism is all about telling people what they need to believe. We approached them with this "I've got something you need, that I'm going to tell you all about, so that you can have it too." And as I finished up this sermon last Friday, at a Starbucks right around the corner from my home, an example of this was being lived out right behind me. I had a first-class seat to an overzealous 'evangelist' trying to convince his latest recruit about the truth of the Bible.

Now let me say right at the outset, as I think I've said before, that having once walked in those circles myself, I appreciate the passion and the perseverance of such people. I have no doubt that they dearly love whatever picture of God it is that they have, and that they are as committed as almost anyone to sharing their version of that God with anyone who will listen. And I respect that. But the condescending nature of the conversation and the inaccuracies that were shared made my head want to explode.

Sadly, that is the nature of so much of the evangelistic world today – it's a top-down, over-and-above, I-know-it-all, western-savior, way of approaching others. And that kind of fervor tends to make our faith into little more than an intellectual exercise: a head thing, that involves knowledge, and mental ascent to a certain set of Biblical or theological truths, that in the long run really fail to help people to connect to the God in which we live and move and have our being.

So this morning, I would like to contend that this 5th affirmation can show us another way to be about the activity of an evangelist. What if we replaced our 'let-me-tell-you-what-I-know' . . . or our 'let-me-give-you-what-I-already-have' way of approaching others, with something else; with something a little more humble and a little less offensive?

I was talking about this in a small group several weeks ago and we considered the model that Jesus used to share his faith. I've shared it with you before but is deserves repeating; and it involves three 'B' words! For Jesus, evangelism was about belonging, behaving, and believing. He welcomed everyone, and gave them a sense of belonging; so that they might experience new life, and a new way of living and behaving in the world; and in the process of all of that, they would learn what they believed about themselves, about God, and about life. And that order was important: belonging, behaving, and believing.

But today, too many of us in the Church have reversed this process. In an approach that can't be much more domineering, we approach people with the opposite agenda. We want to tell them what they need to believe, so that they will learn how to behave, and THEN and only then, can they belong to our elite and guarded communities! It's what I call a 'domination' style of evangelism, and very western. Some might even say it is very American.

And we can't be offended by that. One of the things that many of us just celebrated, on July 4th was our gratitude for being Americans! The list of things afforded us in this life simply because we were lucky enough to be born in this country is immense, and our domination around the world is apparent in countless ways. It's not all that evident in the World Cup, in which we never do very well; but in many other ways, America dominates the world scene. And flawed though we might be, and we must always acknowledge that whenever we talk about our blessings, domination is still the way we operate.

Now whether that's healthy model for our nation to embrace, I will leave to you to decide. But when such a model enters the Church, and when it became the model by which we engage in evangelism, we stray from way of Jesus. For the way of Jesus is never about domination; rather it's about servanthood. And these days in particular, serving others seems to have given way to the powers of domination in ways that are doing tremendous damage to our nation! Which is why it is so crucial for us in the Church to once again, revisit the whole subject of servanthood, particularly as it relates to the ways in which we share our faith.

I have to believe that if James and John knew that this story about their encounter with Jesus was still being told today, they would be completely embarrassed. Because there's no way to tell it, or interpret it, in a manner that doesn't make them look extremely arrogant and egotistical. Scripture tells us in other places that they, along with Peter, were perhaps a little closer to Jesus than the other 9 disciples . . . and here, by asking for the two most important places of honor in the coming kindom, it's like they're just trying rub the faces of their friends in that reality. They're trying to upstage their friends, and to confirm how close to Jesus they really are . . . and how much better they are, than everyone else. And those feelings are exposed for all the world to see, which . . . is rather embarrassing.

Interestingly, when Matthew copies this story, and tells it in his version of the Gospel, he doesn't have James and John asking for these seats of honor. He has their mother, Salome, do it. Mom is the one who is made to look a little arrogant, and pushy. What's new, right moms? You always get the blame, don't you?

But that's Matthew. In Mark. James and John are making the request, and one of the things that makes it particularly awkward is that just prior to this encounter with the Zebedee brothers, Jesus had been talking about humility, and his impending death. So having this kind of a conversation had to have been a little disheartening for him. First, there was not even the slightest bit of humility in their request; and second, the disciples still didn't appear to be even remotely interested in talking with Jesus about his dying. So Jesus had to have wondered when his friends were going to catch on.

They were so painfully clueless, and for so long, that he had to have wondered when they going to realize that in God's kindom, greatness is not measured the way it's measured in the world! It's not determined by how high one is exalted above everyone else; by audacious displays of wealth and power. It's not measured by our ability to dominate, or oppress others; calling people demeaning names, and pushing them down so that we might appear to be lifted up. It's not about the haughty demands of loyalty, or respect, or any definition of greatness that is built on the persecution of others.

Being great, at least according to Jesus, begins with humility and ends with servanthood. And when we think about this in terms of a new model of evangelism, I think it might become not just a little easier, but a little more reflective of, the way of Jesus.

So what if, rather than thinking of sharing our faith as telling people about Jesus or even inviting them to worship . . . what if rather than trying to tactfully broach the subject of faith, or think that we have to be ready to answer all their questions about the Bible, and since we're Presbyterian, predestination . . . what if in place of all that we just learned to see evangelism as caring for others?

I mean think about it. Really think about it! Who are the people in your life to whom God is simply calling you to love, by serving them? And what might that look like? Jesus never calls us to domination. He calls us to lives of servanthood. We know that! At least I think we do, right? Well, think about that in terms of your evangelism.

What it means, is that I don't need to learn everything there is to know about my Muslim or Jewish neighbor's faith; and I don't need to have to figure out how I'm going bring up the subject of Church so that I can invite them to worship. I just need to reach out and serve them. I need to be Christ to them when I see them. I need to take them a few of the cookies that I just baked, or to pick up an extra quart of blueberries at the market. I need to help them carry their groceries in when I see them in their driveway unloading their car.

Friends, what might this look like for you?

Can you picture it? Are you first even able to name a few people who might fall into the category of ones that God has put in your life for whom you simply to care?

Sadly, we live in a culture where domination is encouraged, admired, and rewarded. Everyone seems to be about gaining power and lauding it over everyone else. But that is never the way of the Christ. His life was about washing the dirty feet of his friends. It was about serving others, anyone and everyone who had a need.

In 2021 the Church will celebrate the 100th birthday of the great British theologian John R.W. Stott. He was a pastor and a prolific author, and in talking about the Church's service to others he once said, "It is impossible to be truly converted to God, without being converted to our neighbor."

So friends, this morning, may we be converted to our neighbors! And may we learn to care for them, with an evangelistic fervor that has the capacity to change not just the Church, but the world.

Or to put it in the vernacular, let's just make sure we're smoking, what we're selling.

Reclaiming Jesus: Belief #6
July 15, 2018

Let us build a house where prophets speak, and words are strong and true,
Where all God's children dare to seek to dream God's reign anew.
Here the cross shall stand as witness and as symbol of God's grace;
Here as one we claim the faith of Jesus all are welcome in this place.

Let us build a house where love is found in water, wine, and wheat;
A banquet hall on holy ground where peace and justice meet.
Here the love of God, through Jesus, is revealed in time and space;
As we share in Christ the feast that frees us: all are welcome in this place.

Let us build a house where hands will reach beyond the wood and stone
To heal and strengthen, serve and teach, and live the word they've known.
Here the outcast and the stranger bear the image of God's face;
Let us bring an end to fear and danger: all are welcome in this place
(Let us build a house, vss. 2-4)

Psalm 24 (CEB)

The earth is the LORD's and everything in it, the world and its inhabitants
too.
Because God is the one who established it on the seas;
God set it firmly on the waters.
Who can ascend the LORD's mountain? Who can stand in his holy sanctuary?
Only the one with clean hands and a pure heart;
the one who hasn't made false promises,
the one who hasn't sworn dishonestly.
That kind of person receives blessings from the LORD
and righteousness from the God who saves.
And that's how things are with the generation that seeks him—
that seeks the face of Jacob's God.
Mighty gates: lift up your heads! Ancient doors: rise up high!
So the glorious king can enter!
Who is this glorious king? The LORD—strong and powerful!
The LORD—powerful in battle!
Mighty gates: lift up your heads! Ancient doors: rise up high!
So the glorious king can enter!

Who is this glorious king? The LORD of heavenly forces—
he is the glorious king!

Matthew 28:16-20

Now the eleven disciples went to Galilee, to the mountain where Jesus told them to go. When they saw him, they worshipped him, but some doubted. Jesus came near and spoke to them, "I've received all authority in heaven and on earth. Therefore, go and make disciples of all nations, baptizing them in the name of the Father and of the Son and of the Holy Spirit, teaching them to obey everything that I've commanded you. (And) look, I myself will be with you every day, until the end of this present age."

I haven't been sleeping well for the past 6 weeks! This sermon series has been weighing heavily on my mind, and I have found myself clenching my teeth, waking up in the middle of the night, and just constantly thinking about . . . what **I** wanted to say, what the **Spirit** wanted me to say, and then . . . as the Serenity Prayer goes . . . the wisdom to know the difference. You see I am well aware that not everyone in the Christian Church today sees what is going on in our country as a crisis; and such people are likely to find a new confessional statement completely unnecessary. Others regard all that is going on as God's will: and to some of those people, current events are a blessing, in that we're finally moving closer and closer to God's hope for our nation. And still others believe that current events are being used by the Spirit of God to wake up a silent majority, many of whom are finally finding the courage to speak truth to power.

But in spite of the varied opinions on the role of the Church in our nation's current state of affairs, the vast majority of Christ-followers that I know, both here at Mount Vernon and around our country, are keenly aware that something is very wrong today, and that the Church, and the message of Jesus, have been hijacked. We know that the moral bankruptcy that is being played out on our national stage is unlike anything we've ever seen in any of our lifetimes. Perhaps, it is unlike anything our country has EVER seen: an opinion that, granted, may be taken simply because it is a moral bankruptcy confronting US, and not people in another time and place.

It's not easy being a pastor, or religious leader, these days; because we are the ones called upon to give voice to the concerns of the faith community, and to encourage us all to stand up to ungodliness, especially when it is being passed off as an acceptable ways of thinking about faithfulness and the teachings of Jesus. So this morning I will *cautiously* wrap up this sermon series; but I will do so by again referencing the Serenity Prayer, and being very clear that today my call to you is less about accepting the things we cannot change, and more focused on changing the things we cannot accept. For this is what the "Reclaiming Jesus" movement is all about. And so if you are interested in learning more about it, I would encourage you to go to reclaimingjesus.com.

The "Confession of Faith in a Time of Crisis", that we've been looking at for the past several weeks has six affirmations, and thus far we've looked at the first five. We've considered the Church's oneness in Christ – a oneness that exists regardless of color, ethnicities, genders, or sexual orientations. We've been reminded that Jesus bakes cakes for everyone; and that Scripture calls us to treat immigrants and foreigners with the same kindness and compassion that we show any other citizen. We've looked at why truth matters, and not just in the sense of not bearing false witness – the 9th commandment – telling lies and perpetuating untruths; but further that, what it means to order our lives around THE truth, that we name and know as Jesus. And then last week we looked at 'greatness', and saw that according to Jesus, being great is not about domination, but rather that it begins with humility and ends with servanthood.

Now this morning we're tackling affirmation #6, perhaps the hardest one of all. And it read as follows:

> We believe Jesus when he tells us to go into all nations and make disciples. Our churches and our nations are part of an international community whose interests always surpass national boundaries. (So) we in turn should (then) love and serve the world and all its inhabitants, rather than seek first narrow, nationalistic prerogatives. Therefore, we reject "America First" as a theological heresy for followers of Christ; (for) while we share a patriotic love for our

country, we reject xenophobic or ethnic nationalism that place one nation over others as a political goal.

Now do you know why I'm not sleeping?

Those are hard words for me to utter from this pulpit! Not because I don't believe them, or because it is in any way inappropriate for them to spoken here in a place of Christian worship; but because they point to the countercultural aspect of the Gospel that makes many of us extremely uncomfortable. Most of you I think know that I am quick to say all the time that we are citizens of heaven before we are ever citizens of the United States of America; but rejecting the idea of "America First" – and actually saying that out loud – sounds so harsh, and after recent Fourth of July celebrations, so unpatriotic.

Which is why I feel the need to point out this confession of faith is not born in any kind of disrespect, or resentment towards our country – a country that we ALL love! Rather it comes from a place of honest discernment, as people of faith attempt to wrestle with what it means to truly confess that "Jesus is Lord!" Because that statement challenges the patriotic allegiances of citizens of every country, and it is far more political than we sometimes realize or want to admit.

You see the title 'Lord' is a political title. I know that today we want to think of it as being a spiritual one; but 2000 years ago that was simply not the case. In fact throughout the Bible as a whole, the concept of 'Lord' is extremely political. The title 'King' was also a political title! And these titles, as well as others like them, were given to Jesus because they were the faith community's attempt to say that their allegiance was to God before any Emperor that might be sitting on any earthly throne. That concept was vital to any authentic profession of faith; and so because empire theology was so prevalent, and loyalty to Rome was so strong, Jesus' message was all about shifting peoples' allegiances from the state, to God. So whether we like it or not, the Gospel was, and remains, extremely political.

And this shouldn't surprise any of us; for the words 'religion' and 'politics' have a great deal in common. The Latin word 'religio' means to reconnect, for that's what religion, and spirituality, seek to do – they reconnect us to someone more, something greater, something beyond us! The word 'polis', from which we get the world politics, means city or public forum where people come together and . . . reconnect. Religion and politics are BOTH about people connecting, and how t to actually do that! They address our life together, our life in community, and thus in so many ways they are inseparable.

So while we in this country advocate for the separation of church and state, we do not, we cannot, ever, advocate a separation between faith and politics. If we truly believe that our faith is at the very heart of who we are, then it must impact and affect everything about us, including our politics. So while we may not want to push our Church traditions, rituals, or practices on others, there are basic beliefs that people of all faith hold in common, that when agreed upon, can rightly become law. And that is not forbidden by any American concept of the separation of Church and State. That separation was designed NOT to keep people from exercising moral or ethical propositions, but rather it was designed to safeguard religious freedom, and to ensure that our government would never be dominated by a single religion's practices or traditions. But as far as out faith goes, that MUST impact our politics; because both are all about how we do life together. And for Christ-followers, both must be about the way of Jesus.

Here in the Body of Christ we need to vehemently avoid partisanship, but politics is something else altogether: for the Gospel is nothing, if it's not political! And that's the first thing that needs to be acknowledged as we consider affirmation number six this morning. Scripture's use of political titles for Jesus, and the symbiotic relationship between religion and politics means that as people of faith, as followers of Jesus, we MUST be dealing with the issues surrounding our life together. How we treat others is at the heart of both what it means to religious, and what it means to be political.

Now let's take this a little further. And this is where the matter can become so problematic for some. This 'life together', about which we are called to be concerned, both religiously and politically, knows no boundaries. Jesus tells his disciples to go to ALL the nations, not just to Israel. Why? Because God's concern is for everyone – all people, everywhere. Our faith impacts not just how we treat Americans, but how we treat everyone . . . because . . . we are citizens of God's kindom before we are citizens of America.

So that means that we're not just concerned about the kids over in our nursery this morning; but we're also concerned about the kids who have yet to be united with their parents down on our southern border, and the kids who were just miraculously rescued from that cave in Thailand. We're not just interested in alleviating homelessness in America's inner cities or the unemployment impacting rural America. We also want to address the homelessness on the streets of Moscow, Mumbai, and Manila; and the 95% unemployment rate in Zimbabwe, and the 77% unemployment rate in Burkina Faso. We are not just concerned about American women saying "Me too" and standing up to the sexism here in this country; but we're also called to stand with the women being oppressed in so much of Arab world, and any place where women are still being marginalized and not allowed to have control over their own lives.

You see, we are not just members of the Mount Vernon Presbyterian Church family. We're part of the larger community of Alexandria. We're part of National Capital Presbytery, and a denomination, that exists all around this country . . . and the world. And because Presbyterians are just part of the Church . . . because there are Southern Baptists in Texas, and Mennonites in Pennsylvania; and because there are Coptic Christians in Egypt, and Eastern Orthodox Christians in the Ukraine . . . AND, perhaps more importantly, because a person's faith is really irrelevant when it comes to the way we treat them . . . we need to be thinking about all people, everywhere! We are part of the human family that exists in every corner of the globe, and so we have no choice but to see beyond our national borders. Any action or behavior that in any way does harm to ANYONE, ANYWHERE, even when some would have us believe it is in our 'national interest', must be challenged by the Body of Christ. For our concern is not just for America, but for the world – not just for Americans, but for all of God's children, everywhere!

Friends, our family . . . our siblings in Christ . . . the human family . . . they take us way beyond the redwood forests and the Gulf stream waters. National boarders mean little, if anything, when it comes to the Kindom of God. And that doesn't mean that Christ-followers shouldn't be good Americans, or good citizens of whatever country we may call home; but it does mean that we citizens of God's kindom before we are citizens anywhere else.

Radical? Perhaps!

But since we've looked at the roots of several words this morning, let's consider one more. The word radical comes from the Latin 'radix' which simply means 'root'; and so that which is radical, simply gets to the root of something. Well friends, when it comes to the Gospel, and Jesus' call to go to ALL nations, the root of that challenge is the reality that all people matter to our God. American? Yes! But also Nigerians and Cameroonians, Ecuadorians and Brazilians, Palestinians and Jordanians, Iraqis and Afghanis. And as far as whose first? Well, before we attempt to answer that, we would do well to these words of Jesus: "many who are first will be last, and many who are last, will be first."

So let's go, to all the nations, not with the message of "America First", but with the message that we are all in this together.

Because we are!

And to God be all the glory, Amen.

Part 3:

September 2018 - Palm Sunday 2019

A Different Kind of Armor
September 2, 2018

Rarely has the division within the 'Grand Old' Party been more obvious during the days of Donald Trump, than upon the death of some of our nation's greatest leaders and patriots. The tension between Trump and Republican Party faithfuls was obvious when the 45th President failed to attend the funeral of former First Lady Barbara Bush in April of 2018; and while he attended the funeral of George Bush in November of that same year, again and again Trump debased the office of the President by speaking harshly of the entire Bush family. But Trump's nastiest words were reserved for Senator John McCain, who died on August 25, 2018, the week before this sermon was preached.

Breathe on me breath of God,
Fill me with life anew,
That I may love, what thou doth love
And do what thou would do.
(Breathe on me breath of God, vs. 1)

Proverbs 3:1-10
My children do not forget my teaching, but keep my commands in your heart,
  for they will prolong your life many years and bring you peace and prosperity.
Let love and faithfulness never leave you; bind them around your neck,
  write them on the tablet of your heart.
Then you will win favor and a good name in the sight of God and others.
Trust in the LORD with all your heart and lean not on your own
understanding;
  in all your ways submit to him, and he will make your paths straight.[a]
Do not be wise in your own eyes; fear the LORD and shun evil.
This will bring health to your body and nourishment to your bones.
Honor the LORD with your wealth, with the firstfruits of all your crops;
  then your barns will be filled to overflowing,
  and your vats will brim over with new wine.

Ephesians 6:10-20
Finally, be strengthened by the Lord and his powerful strength. Put on God's armor so that you can make a stand against the tricks of the devil. We aren't fighting against human enemies but against rulers, authorities, forces of cosmic darkness, and spiritual powers of evil in the heavens. Therefore, pick up the full armor of God so that you can stand your ground on the evil day and after you have done everything possible to still stand. So stand with the belt of truth around your waist, justice as your breastplate, and put shoes on your feet so that you are ready to spread the good news of peace. Above all, carry the shield of faith so that you can extinguish the flaming arrows of the evil one. Take the helmet of salvation and the sword of the Spirit, which is God's word.

Offer prayers and petitions in the Spirit all the time. Stay alert by hanging in there and praying for all believers. As for me, pray that when I open my mouth, I'll get a message that confidently makes this secret plan[a] of the gospel known. I'm an ambassador in chains for the sake of the gospel. Pray so that the Lord will give me the confidence to say what I have to say.

Breathe on me breath of God!

Among the many things that my wife and I have learned from our practice of yoga over the past 10 years is the importance of breath. The simple process of breathing is so natural that we rarely think about it . . . unless of course, we can't. Having a cold, asthma, or any issue with our lungs, no doubt, at times, draws our attention to our breath; but in most instances, inhaling and exhaling are things we do without ever even thinking about them. And that's really rather odd, considering how important our breath really is!

Breath is what gives us life. It's what keeps the organs of the human body functioning. It's what keeps our brains active and clear. Without breath, we die! So it seems as though we should be thinking about it all the time. And the practice of yoga has taught me that. It continues to teach me to be more mindful of my breathing; because when we do that, it really DOES become possible to send healing and health to various part of our bodies: to tense muscles, or to aching joints. It allows us to send rest and release to our souls, and relaxation to all those anxieties and fears that that hold us captive and in bondage!

In so many ways life does indeed rise and fall with our breath; so becoming more mindful of it is a valuable spiritual practice. And for we who are part of the faith community, this also means becoming mindful of the breath of God, the 'ruach,' in Hebrew, of the Holy One. Calling upon the Spirit of God to breathe upon us, like we just did in that last hymn, is a powerful plea and a significant request. And I say that because it involves acknowledging that that this is how we can be better equipped for life: life that according to the Scripture passage I just read involves a battle: and not a battle against mere flesh and blood, but against principalities and powers. Life sometimes IS a battle against forces far greater that most of us imagine. And so it is in this holy breath of God, that we find the very things Paul tells us we need to fight this battle. In this closing chapter of Ephesians we discover that the breath of God clothes us with what he refers to as the armor of God; and that armor includes such things as truth to gird our waists, justice to guard our hearts, and faith to protect us from anything that might seek to hurt or destroy us! And these three pieces of armor: truth, justice, and faith, are what I'd like to lift up this morning.

Now most of us, when we think of armor, we think of the iron and steel plates common to the knights of the middle ages. But God's armor is different. And it's unique, particularly for those of us living in a day when armies and military might are at the highest levels in all of human history! You see, God's armor, breathed upon us by the Spirit, is not the kind of armor that trusts in physical strength or power. It doesn't exalt violence in any way, nor does it attempt to minimize the atrocity of war. God's armor, the kind of armor about which Paul speaks, is an armor that defends and protects at a far deeper level. And so there's no iron, or steel, but rather it is made up things like truth, justice, and faith – gifts, tools, or instruments, that have the capacity to defeat anything that might threaten the goodness and the peace of God. They have the capacity to defend and promote the transformation that is at the heart of the Gospel! And friends, when it comes to things like truth, justice, and faith: well, I'm not sure there's anything more needed by the world today.

In a day when alternate facts muddy the waters of honesty and truth-telling; when privileges and prejudices harden peoples' hearts to the justice that Jesus came to proclaim; and when faith becomes so trite and trivial that the transformative power of God is regularly sacrificed on the selfish altars of material gain and economic prosperity: in such a day, we need to be reminded of God's armor. For the things with which the Spirit equips us are far different from those things that we so often seek.

Yesterday the nation remembered the life of John McCain, perhaps one of the most faithful public servants of a generation: a man who gave his all to his country, and who modeled for us all what it means to be patriot. Was he perfect? He was often the first to admit that was not the case at all . . . which is perhaps why he was so often so willing to work with everyone. Because he knew that when it comes to seeking truth, and justice, we are always stronger together! We do better when we work together. And that is a profoundly spiritual principle! That's part of why it's not good for us to be alone; and why when two or three are gathered to together, the divine presence expands and deepens.

On Friday we also celebrated the life of Aretha Franklin, a woman of great faith, whose music was a call to the world to recognize the rights of women, and Blacks, and all those who had been denied the R-E-S-P-E-C-T that all children of God deserve.

These saints taught us much about the armor of God – truth, justice, and faith: and all three are desperately needed today, because they are the only things that can do battle with that which would stand against the kindom of God. And this is not something we wear on the outside of our bodies. Rather, it is armor found inside of us: in our very hearts! For that is where it is planted: in our souls. And when we have the courage to pause, and become mindful of our breath, we CAN become more aware of our having been equipped for the lives we are living.

I'm not sure these words of Abraham Lincoln have ever meant more to so many people than they do today. Perhaps you've heard them before . . . "We will never be destroyed from the outside. If we falter and lose our freedoms, it will be because we destroyed ourselves." Those often-quoted sentiments are not just true of America, of any and every nation of our world; but those sentiments are also true when considering God's beloved community as well. The kindom of God, the faith community of which we are all a part, knows that threats against us come not so much from anyone or anything out there; but rather, the threats come from within in.

These words, attributed to Lincoln, are actually an abbreviation of his actual comments. Listen to what he really said, because his Lyceum Address, as it is best known, was far more profound and poetic. "Shall we expect some transatlantic military giant to step the ocean and crush us at a blow? Never! All the armies of Europe, Asia, and Africa combined, with all the treasures of the earth . . . could not by force take a drink from the Ohio, or make a track on the Blue Ridge . . . At what point then, is the approach of danger to be expected? I answer. If it ever reaches us, it must spring up amongst us; it cannot come from abroad. If destruction be our lot, we must ourselves be its author and finisher."

Friends, without in any way minimizing the power of the sword, or simplistically dismissing the reality of war, the greatest blessings life has to offer – health, wholeness, success, freedom, love, beauty, peace . . . what we know to be God's kindom – they come NOT through traditional means . . . not through violence or war, not through force or domination, not through oppression or persecution. No! Not at all! This violence and force and oppression: THEY are the enemies of the kindom. And our defense against them, the very armor that God, breathed upon us by the spirit, is truth, justice, and faith.

And it would appear that Abraham Lincoln knew this. He understood that that it was matters of the heart that destroy humanity! And so he grasped Paul's command ". . . (to) be strengthened by the Lord and . . . (to) put on God's armor . . . (Because) we aren't fighting against human enemies but against rulers, authorities, forces of cosmic darkness, and spiritual powers of evil." Lincoln seemed to know that we always need to "stand with the belt of truth around our waist, with justice as our breastplate, and . . . that above all, we need to carry the shield of faith."

This morning's passage has all kinds of powerful imagery, and I've only scratched the surface this morning. So I would encourage you to take some time this week to study it a little more, and then join me in making this morning's bold plea, again and again: Breathe on us breathe of God. Send your truth, your justice, and your faith, so that we might do battle with all principalities and powers, so that our lives, and our world, might continue to become a more accurate reflection of the kindom Jesus proclaimed.

Yes! Breathe on us breathe of God, that the Spiritual food you offer this morning, might equip us for this task, thru Jesus the Christ, Amen!

Religious Perspiration
September 16, 2018

While none of us can claim to know what is truly in the heart of Donald Trump, particularly when it comes to racism and xenophobia; nevertheless, at the very least, the first twenty months of his presidency have legitimized racist and xenophobic language and behavior. But in September of 2018, it was his sexism and misogyny that was once again in the headlines.

The extent of President Trump's disrespect for women was put on display for all the world to see when the "Access Hollywood" video was released in 2016, revealing him speaking about women and women's body parts with language that I will not use here. But when Brett Kavanaugh was nominated to fill a seat on Supreme Court vacated by Justice Anthony Kennedy, the world was once again reminded of Donald Trump's disregard for the "voices of women". Christine Blasey Ford's accusations of Sexual Misconduct against Kavanaugh were 'investigated' and deemed to be without merit, and so we now have a second SCOTUS justice who has been accused of inappropriate sexual behavior by women of reputable character and with distinguished professional careers. This sermon came in the midst of these accusations.

Psalm 19

The heavens are telling the glory of God; and the firmament proclaims his handiwork. Day to day pours forth speech, and night to night declares knowledge. There is no speech, nor are there words; their voice is not heard; yet their voice goes out through all the earth, and their words to the end of the world. In the heavens he has set a tent for the sun, which comes out like a bridegroom from his wedding canopy, and like a strong man runs its course with joy. Its rising is from the end of the heavens, and its circuit to the end of them; and nothing is hid from its heat.

The law of the LORD is perfect, reviving the soul;
the decrees of the LORD are sure, making wise the simple;
the precepts of the LORD are right, rejoicing the heart;
the commandment of the LORD is clear, enlightening the eyes;

the fear of the LORD is pure, enduring forever;
the ordinances of the LORD are true and righteous altogether.
More to be desired are they than gold, even much fine gold;
sweeter also than honey, and drippings of the honeycomb.

Moreover by them is your servant warned;
in keeping them there is great reward.
But who can detect their errors? Clear me from hidden faults.
Keep back your servant also from the insolent;
do not let them have dominion over me.
Then I shall be blameless, and innocent of great transgression.

Let the words of my mouth and the meditation of my heart
be acceptable to you, O LORD, my rock and my redeemer.

James 1:22-27, 2:14-20 (The Message)

Don't fool yourself into thinking that you are a listener when you are anything but, letting the Word go in one ear and out the other. Act on what you hear! Those who hear and don't act are like those who glance in the mirror, walk away, and two minutes later have no idea who they are, or what they look like.

But all who catch a glimpse of the revealed counsel of God—the free life!—even out of the corner of their eye, and stick with it, is no distracted scatterbrain but a man or woman of action. That person will find delight and affirmation in the action.

Those who set themselves up as "religious" by talking a good game are self-deceived. That kind of religion is hot air and only hot air. Real religion, the kind that passes muster before God is this: Reach out to the homeless and loveless in their plight, and guard against corruption from the godless world.

Dear friends, do you think you'll get anywhere in this if you learn all the right words but never DO anything? Does merely talking about faith indicate that a person really has it? For instance, you come upon an old friend dressed in rags and half-starved and say, "Good morning, friend! Be clothed in Christ! Be filled with the Holy Spirit!" and (then) walk off without providing so much as a coat or a cup of soup—where does that get you? Isn't it obvious that God-talk without God-acts is outrageous nonsense?
I can already hear one of you agreeing by saying, "Sounds good. You take care of the faith department; I'll handle the works department."

Not so fast. You can no more show me your works apart from your faith than I can show you my faith apart from my works. Faith and works, works and faith, fit together hand in glove.

Do I hear you professing to believe in the one and only God, but then observe you complacently sitting back as if you had done something wonderful? That's just great. Demons do that, but what good does it do them? Use your heads! Do you suppose for a minute that you can cut faith and works in two and not end up with a corpse on your hands?

This morning's passage is why I so love the Book of James, especially Eugene Peterson's translation in "The Message!" "Don't let the word go in one ear and out the other . . . ACT! . . . those who set themselves up as religious by talking a good game . . . (that's) hot air! . . . real religion reaches out to the homeless . . . and guards against corruption from the godless world . . . faith and works fit together like hand in glove."

James' letter really is letter about a faith, that works! For that is the only faith, that works! And it is at the heart of that phrase that we've begun to use a lot around here – about not just "going to church," but actually "BEING the Church!"

Now what on earth that has to do with religious perspiration . . . the supposed title of this sermon, that I came up with months ago . . . I have absolutely no idea? All I can conclude is that it was probably one of those days where we had the furnace on to reduce the humidity in this building, and I was hot, which is normal for me from like April thru November. So just ignore that title this morning; and if by chance you are here because you saw the sign out front and were intrigued, I'm sorry to disappoint you! My intent was not false advertising!

Faith that works! *That* is the message of James.

If you were here last week when we kicked off this series, you know that James was a leader of the church in Jerusalem. And because of that location, it is believed that James was likely ministering to Jews, who were already religious. While Paul was traveling around the empire focusing on Gentiles, many of whom likely had little, if any kind of religious background: James was dealing with th Jewish people in Jerusalem, helping them to discover Jesus as the promised Messiah, the one who would inaugurate a new reign of God in the world. And Jews, especially Jews in Jerusalem, were very religious. They were practitioners of dietary laws and Sabbath keepers, eager to maintain all kinds of outward signs of their faith.

And it is precisely that kind of religiosity that concerned James. He was worried that their faith had become nothing more than a bunch of rote rites and empty rituals, a philosophical head trip preoccupying them with thoughts about a God, out there, who would occasionally step into this life to work a miracle or two, but who would then retreat to the heavens and leave people alone. They believed that if they just followed the religious laws that had been given to them, everything would be fine!

But James knew that Jesus came to teach us a different way: a way that was all about a world we called to build and community we were made to create. As Jesus' brother, James grew up with Jesus; and so he saw the way Jesus lived; the way he cared for others. When they were little, maybe in Hebrew School, I have to believe that James saw that the way Jesus treated other kids, was different. And he noticed that; and took note. As teenagers, I have to believe that James saw the way his brother behaved, and it had a profound impact on him. And when they were grown men, and Jesus began his ministry, James was aware of how Jesus responded to the woman caught in the act of adultery, the blind man, the leper, the woman at the well, the very disciples who betrayed and denied Him. James watched his older brother every day, and he saw the way he valued people, all people, not just those who looked a certain way, or who believed certain things; not just those who had attained a certain station in life, or who had achieved a certain level of social standing. Jesus valued everyone, and James saw that . . . every day.

Richard Rohr wrote in a recent daily devotional that much of what Jesus taught seems to have been followed closely during the early years of the church. And that was because of people like James.

Now granted, it was easier to do that back then. You see, prior to the time of Constantine – when being a "Christian" became acceptable in the kingdom, almost aligning the Church with the State – in those early years, people had to care for one another; because no one else was doing that. They had to rely on one another, share, show kindness, and compassion, and really DO life together. And so that's what they did. Jesus' example truly was "The Way", and it was how people sought to live.

But then, something happened. By the time the fourth century rolled around, the Church's power had increased, but its witness. . .. well some would say that was precisely when the Church's witness began to decrease! And many believe that has continued until today. In the 4th century the church grew and gained immense power; but it is precisely because of that power the church's theology began to change. It altered our life together and began offering a counterfeit Gospel that still tempts the Body today. And it's clearly one of the reasons the Church is struggling like it is. Things like the sexual abuse scandal in the Roman Church today are merely scratching the surface of a faith community that continues to struggle to understand and live the Gospel message. Today, at least here in America, we have as much money and power and influence as ever, and yet we continue to struggle, because it's all surface!

And that's why James' little letter is so important; for it takes us to the heart of Jesus' life, death, and resurrection: all of which were about the call to love God, by loving God's creation! Faith is simply NOT about rites and rituals; and until we understand that, until the Church understands that there is a direct relationship between loving God and loving the creation of God, the world will continue to suffer. You simply cannot separate the two: loving God, and loving God's creation!

Over the years my kids have created all kinds of things, and not all of them are the most attractive. But because my kids created them, I love them. I noticed this the last time I was at my in-laws' home in Denmark. While my wife's parents have not spent nearly as much time with our kids as Jeanne and I would like, our kids are deeply loved by them. And you don't need to spend too much time with them to find evidence of that. They love all of their grandchildren, and it's obvious in all kinds of ways; from the stories they tell, to the prayers they say, to the things in their home. Among other things, beside their computer is a mouse pad with a picture that was drawn by their oldest Danish grandchild, my son Stefan; and on a shelf above that desk is a bowl that Kirsten made for them when she was in high school. Like so many parents and grandparents, they treasure such objects. My father-in-law has traveled around the world, doing mission work in exotic places: Nepal, Armenia, and Tajikistan; but I don't think any of his souvenirs, from any of those places, mean as much as the creations of his grandkids. A few come close, but not many! And why? Because how we treat a child's masterpiece, reflects how we feel about the child!

How many of you have treasures created by someone you love prominent in your home, or office?

Well that's really this morning's message in a nutshell today. Have you put the pieces to this puzzle together?

Church, the way we treat the world, and everything in it, reveals the depth of our love for God! And since the apex of God's creative activity was revealed in the creation of humanity: people like you and me. And the way we treat one another reveals how we feel about God. Those are the works that James is getting at in this morning's passage. The 'works' to which we are called as followers of Jesus, are all about how we are treating the children of God, particularly the least of these: those who are hungry, or naked, those who are lonely or without family, those who are orphaned, or oppressed, or who are in any way being denied the basics necessities of life. And in light of all that is going on in our nation's capital this week, and as hard as it is to believe, women . . . half of population of this country we all love – must also be named in this group!

Author and pastor Rob Bell writes in his provocatively titled book "Sex God", that whenever a human being is "mistreated, objectified, or neglected . . . when they are treated as less than human, these actions are against God. Because how we treat the creation, reflects how we feel about the Creator." Friends, how we treat women, is how we treat God! Those familiar words . . . when you have done it to the least of these, you have done it unto me . . . James knew what Jesus meant when he made that statement! When you have done it unto women, you have done it unto me. Faith and works go together like hand in glove. Or, as written in a slightly different translation . . . just as the body without the spirit is dead, so faith without deeds, as dead!

Friends, Jesus said, "you cannot love me, and hate your brothers and your sisters." So, how are YOU doing that? How are YOU loving your brothers and sisters? How are WE showing our affection for the Creator, by caring for creation? I know we can't do everything, but we have to do . . . something! Because this is what our faith is all about. It's what the CHURCH, is all about!

This morning remember that popsicle stick napkin holder your son made in preschool; or that pillowcase that your daughter made while she was a way at summer camp. Consider the creations of those you love. But then consider another creation – God's creation – God's people, who are hungry, hurting, and hopeless; and ask yourself this important question: am I more committed to GOING to church, or to BEING the church? Because faith without works is dead. They go together . . . like hand in glove!

A Bigger Table
January 6, 2019

The 2018 midterm elections were held on November 6, and votes were being cast in national races for 35 of the 100 seats in the United States and for all 435 in the United States House of Representatives. In a rebuff of the President that was surprisingly larger than most pundits predicted, Democrats gained 41 seats in the House, and would eventually return its control to Nancy Pelosi, arguably the most powerful woman in America. This was significant not only because Trump would now be forced to work with a divided Congress, but because one of the leaders of Congress was a strong, articulate, and influential . . . woman!

This sermon was preached in 'first-person' format, a format I've been using since I was ordained in 1986. Once or twice a year I will take on the character of a person in the Bible and attempt to preach from their perspective. This is one of those sermons.

Let our hearts not be hardened to those living on the margins
There is room at the table for everyone.
This is where it all begins, this is how we gather in
There is room at the table for everyone.

No matter who you are, no matter where you're from
There is room at the table for everyone.
Here and now we can be, the beloved community
There is room at the table for everyone.
(Room at the table, vss. 1 & 3)

Psalm 23
The LORD is my shepherd, I shall not want.
He makes me lie down in green pastures; he leads me beside still waters;
*   he restores my soul.*
He leads me in right paths for his name's sake.

Even though I walk through the darkest valley,
  I fear no evil; for you are with me;
  your rod and your staff — they comfort me.
You prepare a table before me in the presence of my enemies;
  you anoint my head with oil; my cup overflows.
Surely goodness and mercy shall follow me all the days of my life,
  and I shall dwell in the house of the LORD *my whole life long.*

Mark 2:13-17

Jesus went out again beside the sea; the whole crowd gathered around him, and he taught them. As he was walking along, he saw Levi son of Alphaeus sitting at the tax booth, and he said to him, "Follow me." And he got up and followed him.

And as he sat at dinner in Levi's house, many tax collectors and sinners were also sitting with Jesus and his disciples—for there were many who followed him. When the scribes of the Pharisees saw that he was eating with sinners and tax collectors, they said to his disciples, "Why does he eat with tax collectors and sinners?"

When Jesus heard this, he said to them, "Those who are well have no need of a physician, but those who are sick; I have come to call not the righteous but sinners."

It started like any other day; but with one encounter, one call, everything changed. And nothing in my life would ever be the same again. I was doing what I did everyday: I was collecting taxes! Rome expected me to take in a certain amount of money every day; and I had to add enough on top of what they required to skim off some for myself so that I could survive. Which . . . is why I was so hated . . . by everyone! My bosses in Rome were skeptical of me because I was Jewish, and the Jews didn't like me because they thought I was selling out to the Gentiles by working for the government. But I needed to make a living, didn't I? I needed to survive! I had to work! And if I hadn't taken this job, some other Jew would have! So at least I was somewhat sympathetic to the plight of my people. I didn't rob them as much as I could have, as much as most of the other tax collectors! But that didn't matter. I was lumped together with everyone else and viewed as the enemy!

Which is precisely why Mark writes about me: Levi, also known as Matthew! You see, he was trying to make a point about the way we treat our enemies. Because if anyone was seen as an enemy of the Jews, and thus to Jesus, it was me.

Some people believe that I'm the same guy who wrote another Gospel – you know, the one 'according to Mathew.' But does it really matter? Many of us had a hand in the writing of everything that you call Scriptures today. Many of us had spent a great deal of time with Jesus, and those of us who didn't actually know him . . . well, we still *knew* him! So after he was killed, we all had stories to tell. We all had individual memories, and we all wanted our experiences to be remembered. Over time, sure, they were modified and changed, usually to drive home one message or another. But in the end, you wound up with a bunch of different accounts of the Gospel story . . . ALL pointing to Jesus! So while the Gospels that you read today may not be factual in each and every detail, they still . . . they still have great power and wisdom; and most important, they still reveal the unique and unparalleled love that we saw in Jesus, the Christ: the child born to Mary, the one visited by shepherds and kings, the one who would one day grow up and . . . save the world from itself.

Anyway, back to my story! I actually take great pride in the fact that my story is told in three of the four of gospels. That's how significant my story is! And it's important because I was so hated. We tax-collectors might have been likened to . . . fathers who don't make their child support payments, or to mothers who use their welfare checks to buy drugs rather than formula! I was right up there with guys who cheat on their wives and used car salesmen. So needless to say, life was hard for me! It was no fun being on the margins of a society: being looked down upon, rejected by family, and without any real friends. Even those I had known all of my life wanted nothing to do with me.

But Jesus? . . . he was different. Jesus seemed to intuitively understand what this was like. Or, maybe it was because it was beginning to happen to him. I mean just consider what was going on his ministry began to grow. He was slowly being shut out of the synagogue. He was slowly being excluded from the temple. And so the open air - on the hillside or beside the lake - places like that, we're becoming his . . . church. How ironic is that? The son of God, banned from the house of God – what is wrong with that picture?

As a result, Jesus knew what it was like to be considered an enemy . . . an outsider. . . maybe that's why when he saw me, he called me as quickly as he did. I know it's why I responded as quickly as I did! I could tell that here was a man who was going to treat me like a friend, a brother, part of the family. And so as a result, my heart was moved. Something in me clicked and my day . . . a day which had started like any other, had changed! Over time, as I listened to all Jesus had to say, and as I learned how he was calling us to live our lives, I was will willing to give up everything to follow him. And that was not an easy decision, I assure you.

I know the text makes it sound like I made this decision quickly, but I didn't; and it was not easy! You see once I agreed to follow him, I knew that there was no going back. All of my bridges were burned as soon as I told Rome that I was done! And so I had now alienated BOTH the Jews, AND Rome; and I was about as alone as one could get. And to make matters worse, when I began inviting the other outcasts of society to my home for dinner: well that pretty much sealed my fate. At that point I was rejected by everyone!

But ya' know what? I just didn't care. Knowing Jesus, following Jesus . . . made it all worthwhile.

So eventually Jesus' message became my own. The Scribes and Pharisees, all the supposed spokespeople for the faith community, the religious blabbermouths of the day - I came to see that they were all really pretty clueless. You know what those people are like, don't you? They THINK they speak for the Church, but they don't. And the message that they offer is nothing at all like the one Jesus offered.

Jesus? Well, Jesus loved everyone: especially the outcasts, and the ones labeled enemies, or unacceptable. In the Gospel that some believe I wrote, the genealogy of Jesus includes four women, people that most think had questionable moral character! But they . . . WE . . . are the people Jesus came to reach: the people he came to touch, and to transform, and to offer the gift of resurrection. We are ones he came to save! Because while, of course, he loves and cares for everyone; there is none the less a special place in the heart of Jesus for people like me.

Fortunately, you do have a few preachers today reminding you that peoples' worth and value are not dependent on what they make, or produce, or own, or accomplish. That's simply not the way it works with God. At God's table, there is always room for everyone. Like the big holiday gatherings some of you just enjoyed, when Jesus was around, leaves had to be put in the table to make room for everyone. That's just the way it is with Jesus!

Yeah! It started like any other day, but with that one encounter, with that one call, everything changed. After meeting Jesus, nothing in my life would ever be the same again.

So how about you? You just finished celebrating his birth, and you do that so well! But has he really changed you? Today is the day that many people celebrate what is called the Feast of Epiphany: the visit of the magi to the home of Mary, Joseph, and Jesus. Churches and pastors everywhere will talk about giving our hearts to Jesus . . . but do you know what that really means?

Giving our hearts to Jesus means that we then take his heart, as our own. And that means at we need to start loving those he loves - everyone, yes - but especially your enemies, especially those on the margins of your society: the White supremacist, the old white guy in the MAGA hat, the immigrant, the refugee, the FOX reporter, the fundamentalist Christian, the Muslim extremist, the climate-change-denier, that CEO making more money in a month than some of us will make in a lifetime . . . you fill in the blank. They are the people we are all called to love: because they, our enemies, those on the margins of our society . . . are the ones Jesus came to save. An so they must have a place at the table! We may not like all of them. And they may need to be challenged and held accountable for attitudes and behavior that deny the Gospel. But friends, there is always room at this table, for all of them, and for all, of us!

This New Year has started like any other new year. So is anything going to change? Most of you have met Jesus. So, are you changing? Are you any different this January 6th than you were last January 6th?

I sure hope so. Because if not, then what are we doing here? If not, then what is all this about?

It was a day like any other day, but when Jesus called me – Mathew – everything changed. When he made room at the table for me, everything changed. And that's what Jesus was all about, changing the lives of people on the margins.

It's what HE gave his life TO. It's what he gave his life FOR!

What about you?

The Life of Moses: Biblical Bra-Burners
January 27, 2019

O n Friday of the week prior to my preaching this sermon, the longest government shut down in American history came to an end. As the second anniversary of Trump's inauguration comes and goes, he and many in his party continue to tear at the very fabric of the nation. Rep. Steve King (R-Iowa) continues his pattern of justifying and at times praising White Supremacy; and President Trump, while continuing to manufacture a fear of immigrants, declares he has a 'major announcement' regarding his boarder wall. The announcement was a declaration that the situation along our southern border was a 'national disaster' and thus, as President, he intended to use "Disaster Relief Funds" to pay for . . . what he no longer calling a wall, but rather a "barrier"!

The next two sermons are part of a series on the life of Moses, and both deal with issues similar to many of the issues facing our nation during the presidency of Donald Trump.

Exodus 1:8-22

Now a new king arose over Egypt, who did not know Joseph. He said to his people, "Look, the Israelite people are more numerous and more powerful than we. Come, let us deal shrewdly with them, or they will increase and, in the event of war, join our enemies and fight against us and escape from the land." Therefore they set taskmasters over them to oppress them with forced labor. They built supply cities, Pithom and Rameses, for Pharaoh. But the more they were oppressed, the more they multiplied and spread, so that the Egyptians came to dread the Israelites. The Egyptians became ruthless in imposing tasks on the Israelites and made their lives bitter with hard service in mortar and brick and in every kind of field labor. They were ruthless in all the tasks that they imposed on them.

The king of Egypt said to the Hebrew midwives, one of whom was named Shiphrah and the other Puah, "When you act as midwives to the Hebrew women, and see them on the birthstool, if it is a boy, kill him; but if it is a girl, she shall live." But the midwives feared God; they did not do as the king of Egypt commanded them, but they let the boys live. So the king of Egypt summoned the midwives and said to them, "Why have you done this, and allowed the boys to live?" The midwives said to Pharaoh, "Because the Hebrew women are not like the Egyptian women; for they are vigorous and give birth before the midwife comes to them." So God dealt well with the midwives; and the people multiplied and became very strong. And because the midwives feared God, he gave them families. Then Pharaoh commanded all his people, "Every boy that is born to the Hebrews you shall throw into the Nile, but you shall let every girl live."

Exodus 2:1-10

Now a man from the house of Levi went and married a Levite woman. The woman conceived and bore a son; and when she saw that he was a fine baby, she hid him three months. When she could hide him no longer, she got a papyrus basket for him, and plastered it with bitumen and pitch; she put the child in it and placed it among the reeds on the bank of the river. His sister stood at a distance, to see what would happen to him.

The daughter of Pharaoh came down to bathe at the river, while her attendants walked beside the river. She saw the basket among the reeds and sent her maid to bring it. When she opened it, she saw the child? He was crying, and she took pity on him. "This must be one of the Hebrews' children," she said. Then his sister said to Pharaoh's daughter, "Shall I go and get you a nurse from the Hebrew women to nurse the child for you?" Pharaoh's daughter said to her, "Yes." So the girl went and called the child's mother. Pharaoh's daughter said to her, "Take this child and nurse it for me, and I will give you your wages." So the woman took the child and nursed it. When the child grew up, she brought him to Pharaoh's daughter, and she took him as her son. She named him Moses, "because," she said, "I drew him out of the water."

Moses – one of the greatest leaders the faith community has ever seen is known to all three of the world's largest religions as a great pastor, preacher, prophet, and priest. He was a strong and devout servant leader, with life experiences that over and over again, put him on holy ground: whether barefoot before a burning bush, or sandal clad on the peaks of Mt. Sinai. Moses always seemed to be profoundly aware of God's presence in the world, but it would take a little time for him to become aware of God's presence in his own life.

Now when most people think of Moses – at least most people over the age of 40, we think of Charlton Heston, right? Under the age of 40 . . . well, if you weren't raised in the church, when you think of Moses you likely think of either basketball player Moses Malone, or Moses Brown. Perhaps you just think of Disney's Prince of Egypt, released back in 1998; in which case you might simply lump him together with Gaston from Beauty and the Beast, or Prince Naveen from The Princess and the Frog. But the Moses of the Bible is so very much more, and over the next few weeks we're going to delve into the stories of his life, and see why people everywhere, from film studios to seminaries, are so powerfully moved by accounts of his life!

Our second Scripture reading for the day tells us of his birth, and how for several months he was hidden by his mother Jochebed, in fear that he might be killed by Pharaoh's minions. Eventually, when she realizes that she can't keep him any longer without threatening both of their lives, she puts him in a basket, and sends him down the Nile River so that he might be found by Pharaoh's daughter, who Jochebed likely knew would take him into the palace and raise him as her own.

But before we get too far ahead of ourselves, and jump into all the events that shaped Moses' life, we need to spend a little more time considering his birth: because most likely, Moses would not have survived were it not for the faithful midwives referenced in this morning's first Scripture reading. Without THEIR story, there wouldn't likely not even BE, a MOSES story!

So let's transport ourselves back in time, so that we might consider what is going on in Egypt. The Hebrew immigrants: the descendants of Joseph, who had been harshly enslaved in Egypt, and who were working at jobs no one else wanted, were very simply, taking over. With what some might today call 'anchor babies', their numbers were growing, and they were beginning to challenge the privileged, ruling minority. Life in Egypt had begun to change, and that reality was scaring the Egyptians. Their old, traditional way of doing things was being challenged, and slowly but surely the nation was changing.

So, what did Pharaoh do? He began stoking fear in the hearts of his people – a fear that would lead them, as fear always does, to behave in unGodly ways. And his plan was very simple.

In order to quell the rising tide of Hebrew power and influence, the anxious but shrewd Egyptian king called a press conference to make a 'a major announcement'! And that announcement is an absurd and insecure decree that all the midwives in the land – the women who were present to help the Hebrew women when they would go into labor – are to kill all the male babies that are born, across the land.

Chuck Swindoll, in his book on Moses, written back in the late 1990s, offered words that he no doubt regrets today. He said back then, "The Egyptians wallowed in fear . . . fear of loss, fear of weakness, fear of losing control . . . and that drove them to ever more vicious acts of injustice. Because once you've decided to mistreat one person," Swindoll says, "it becomes easy to persecute a whole population."

This was precisely how the Egyptian king was behaving. But fortunately, there were two women, two midwives, Shiphrah and Puah, who had a conscience: and a courageous one at that! These great women of faith were able to discern what kind of behavior is of God what kind is not, and so along with other women of God scattered all around the country, they decide to quietly stand up to the king and defy his decree! They knew that the laws of God always come before human laws: before the laws of nations and nationalists, before the laws of parliaments . . . and presidents.

Now needless to say, when Pharaoh notices that the Hebrew population was continuing to grow and expand, he called the midwives together again to inquire about what was happening! And their response?

"Well, we don't really know! It just appears as though the Hebrew women are not like Egyptian women! They're more 'vigorous' in childbirth" – whatever that means – "and so as a result, their babies are born before the we midwives can ever get there!"
It's such a familiar story isn't it? And sadly, and painfully relevant!

As is so often the case, when people UNlike us increase in numbers, and bring new customs and colors, when they expose us to differences and diversity . . . that with which we are just not familiar, people become frightened! And as we've seen in previous studies, such fear can lead even the most faithful people of God, to turn from compassion to contempt! Our fears, unreasonable and irrational though they may be, blind us to reality; and so we trade truth for lies, imagining the worst about others, and making potential friends into perceived enemies.

However, the Spirit is always present in the midst of these challenges! There are always people around who have the wisdom, and the faith, and the conviction, to soothe the fear and to challenge the injustice. And in Moses' day, it was the midwives. Perhaps like so many women from the 1960's, who were not afraid to push back against the patriarchy of our culture, the mid-wives of Exodus were the Biblical bra-burners of their day; and Moses came into this world precisely because of their faithfulness to the ways of God!

You see like most great leaders, Moses stood on the shoulders of countless obedient women and men who had come before him. And while leaders may indeed have a certain measure of giftedness that we cannot ignore, they don't do whatever they do, or accomplish whatever they accomplish, without the help of those who came before them . . . people who did the groundwork and laid the foundation for those leaders' ministries! And Moses was no different. So before we can even begin to look at his life, we need to acknowledge and celebrate the midwives: particularly, Shiphrah and Puah – two names, that most Christ-followers don't even know, but should!

Shiphrah and Puah! Say them with me . . . Shiphrah and Puah!

This morning's story is about how several thousand years ago, these original bra-burners put on the pink pussy hats of their day – whatever they may have been – and were not afraid to challenge the mandates of men, the commands of kings, or the proclamations of presidents, that they KNEW were about nothing more than the fearful and unjust oppression of others. And so they defied the laws of their land and instead sought to be obedient to the will and way of God.

Now as we think about these women – as we reflect on the lives of Shiphrah and Puah – we may be inclined to think that they were specially gifted and uniquely equipped to be God's person in their world. And we likely think that way because as author and musician David LaMotte shared with us last September, the stories of our culture are ones that only allow for those blessed with supposed super-powers to become the heroes, right? We are led to believe that only super people, have superpowers. Superman was able to leap tall buildings in a single bound. Wonder Woman was an unconquerable warrior of the Amazons. And the Black Panther's strength, stamina, and speed were all . . . superhuman, like a panther!

And this is because so many of the typical American hero stories are all about the exception, doing the exceptional. But folks, those stories are not reality! And we see that in this morning's story from Exodus – in the story of the midwives.

Those women didn't have any more gifts or abilities than any of us. And just as they, Shiphrah and Puah, had the power and the capacity to change their stories, and the narrative of life for the Hebrews in Egypt, so too do we! You see, again, as reminded us last year, it is not unreasonable to think that we can change the world! Rather, it is unreasonable for us to think that we can live in this world and not change it! We're all changing the world all the time – all of us. History proves that the traditional hero story is actually not the norm. History reveals that more often than not, the real heroes of our society and culture are average people, like you and me, who simply find within themselves the strength and the courage to do the right thing!

If you've not yet seen the movie "On the basis of sex" about Supreme Court Justice Ruth Bader Ginsburg, I encourage you do check it out. It's worth it simply for the final couple of scenes. That is when she is testifying before the Colorado Court of Appeals; and the three old white male judges are concerned because they think she is asking the court to change the country through their legislation: something many are inclined to still warn us against today. But when the justices express their concerns, notorious RBG quietly, and humbly, and dispassionately declares "if it pleases the court . . . we're not asking you to change the country, that's already happened without any court's permission. We're simply asking you to acknowledge the right of the country to change!"

I love that scene because it reminds us that those in power rarely change the world. It's average people, like you and me, who change things. People you've likely never heard of, but whose lives give testimony and witness to nothing more than divine obedience.

Church, contrary to what we've been led to believe, the world is NOT changed by famous people doing great big things. And history gives testimony to this reality! Malaysian social activist Anwar Fazal says, "it's LITTLE people, doing LITTLE things, in LITTLE places everywhere, that change the world."

If you've seen the news this weekend, then you've likely heard about Anthony Maggert. He's is the vet who lost a leg in Afghanistan, and while driving on the beltway last week, saw a car pulled over on the side of the road, with the driver trying to change a tire. Well Anthony pulled over to try and help, and it turned out that the guy struggling with his lug nuts was none other than Colin Powell.

Later, reflecting on the experience, Colin said, "these are the things that make a country great. People just being kind and taking care of one another." Anthony and Colin are two people who, just by looking at them you can see, do not have very much in common. Besides being vets, their lives are as different as night and day. But that didn't prevent Anthony from pulling over on the side of the road, in order to help someone in need.

A small, great thing! That's really all we're called to do. Small, great things!

This friends, is where the story of Moses begins: with the midwives' small, great things! May that be how we move into tomorrow: with hearts set on doing small, great things!

The Life of Moses: Silence is Consent

February 3, 2019

Exodus 2:11-25

One day, after Moses had grown up, he went out to his people and saw their forced labor. He saw an Egyptian beating a Hebrew, one of his kinsfolk. He looked this way and that and seeing no one he killed the Egyptian and hid him in the sand. When he went out the next day, he saw two Hebrews fighting; and he said to the one who was in the wrong, "Why do you strike your fellow Hebrew?" He answered, "Who made you a ruler and judge over us? Do you mean to kill me as you killed the Egyptian?" Then Moses was afraid and thought, "Surely the thing is known." When Pharaoh heard of it, he sought to kill Moses.

But Moses fled from Pharaoh. He settled in the land of Midian and sat down by a well. The priest of Midian had seven daughters. They came to draw water and filled the troughs to water their father's flock. But some shepherds came and drove them away. Moses got up and came to their defense and watered their flock. When they returned to their father Reuel, he said, "How is it that you have come back so soon today?" They said, "An Egyptian helped us against the shepherds; he even drew water for us and watered the flock." He said to his daughters, "Where is he? Why did you leave the man? Invite him to break bread." Moses agreed to stay with the man, and he gave Moses his daughter Zipporah in marriage. She bore a son, and he named him Gershom; for he said, "I have been an alien residing in a foreign land."

Exodus 3:1-15

Moses was keeping the flock of his father-in-law Jethro, the priest of Midian; he led his flock beyond the wilderness, and came to Horeb, the mountain of God. There the angel of the LORD appeared to him in a flame of fire out of a bush; he looked, and the bush was blazing, yet it was not consumed. Then Moses said, "I must turn aside and look at this great sight and see why the bush is not burned up." When the LORD saw that he had turned aside to see, God called to him out of the bush, "Moses, Moses!" And he said, "Here I am." Then he said, "Come no closer! Remove the sandals from your feet, for the place on which you are standing is holy ground." He said further, "I am the God of your father, the God of Abraham, the God of Isaac, and the God of Jacob." And Moses hid his face, for he was afraid to look at God.

Then the LORD said, "I have observed the misery of my people who are in Egypt; I have heard their cry on account of their taskmasters. Indeed, I know their sufferings, and I have come down to deliver them from the Egyptians, and to bring them up out of that land to a good and broad land, a land flowing with milk and honey, to the country of the Canaanites, the Hittites, the Amorites, the Perizzites, the Hivites, and the Jebusites. The cry of the Israelites has now come to me; I have also seen how the Egyptians oppress them. So come, I will send you to Pharaoh to bring my people, the Israelites, out of Egypt." But Moses said to God, "Who am I that I should go to Pharaoh, and bring the Israelites out of Egypt?" He said, "I will be with you; and this shall be the sign for you that it is I who sent you: when you have brought the people out of Egypt, you shall worship God on this mountain."

But Moses said to God, "If I come to the Israelites and say to them, 'The God of your ancestors has sent me to you,' and they ask me, 'What is his name?' what shall I say to them?" God said to Moses, "I AM WHO I AM." He said further, "Thus you shall say to the Israelites, 'I AM has sent me to you.'" God also said to Moses, "Thus you shall say to the Israelites, 'The LORD, the God of your ancestors, the God of Abraham, the God of Isaac, and the God of Jacob, has sent me to you': This is my name forever, and this my title for all generations.

> *Deep in the shadows of the past, far out from settled lands,*
> *Some nomads traveled with their God, across the desert sands.*
> *The dawn of hope for humankind, was glimpsed by them alone:*
> *A promise calling them ahead, a future yet unknown.*
>
> *While others bowed to changeless gods, they met a mystery:*
> *God with an uncompleted name, "I am what I will be";*
> *And by their tents, around their fires, in story, song, and law*
> *They praised, remembered, handed on a past that promised more.*

These Brian Wren lyrics, that were just shared with us from a new hymn in our hymnal, are part of a brooding piece of poetry about Scripture: where it came from, how it was passed along, and to whom it sought to point. Ours is indeed, a faith born in stories, song, and law; and few stories have had a greater impact on the growth and development of the world's three largest Abrahamic religions than those involving Moses. And while there always has been and likely always will be a great deal of debate about whether or not he is a 'historical' figure or a 'legendary' figure, either way he is a man who has a great deal to teach us.

That hymn continues . . .

> *From Abraham to Nazareth the promise changed and grew,*
> *While some, remembering the past, recorded what they knew,*
> *And some, in letters or laments, in prophecy and praise,*
> *Recovered, held, and re-expressed new hope for changing days.*
>
> *For all the writings that survived, for leaders, long ago,*
> *Who sifted, chose, and then preserved the Bible that we know,*
> *Give thanks, and find its promise yet our comfort, strength, and call,*
> *The working model for our faith, alive with hope for all.*

A model for our faith! Hope for all! That's what Moses' life was all about. Whether a man or a myth, his stories, like the one just read for us from Exodus chapter 2 reveal a man who refused to be silent in the face of injustice. And that kind of faithfulness should inspire US to so live, and it should give all the world great hope. That baby who was left in the hands of Pharaoh's daughter last week, after having been saved at birth by the faithfulness of the midwives, that baby has now grown up to become the truth-teller that his people need.

Raised with the children of Pharaoh, privileged and prosperous, Moses eventually discovers his Hebrew roots, and realizes that he had been living a lie! He was not the man the people thought he was; but rather a descendant of the very people who were being enslaved by the ones who had raised him. And this realization would forever alter the trajectory of Moses' life. It would change his heart in profound ways and push him to become the prophet and the leader that God was calling him to be.

Seeing the misery and abuse of his people, Moses' heart was broken; and witnessing their enslavement, day after day, eventually becomes too hard for him to handle. He realizes that remaining silent in the face of such injustice was no better than giving overt consent to it; and so what we see in this morning's first Scripture reading is his breaking point. When he sees an Egyptian beating

146

one of his kinsman, he kills the man, and in so doing gives away his identity. So, he realizes that he needs to leave Egypt, and thus sets out to begin a new life away from both Pharaoh and his people.

And . . . where does he go?

Well, he goes where people in the Bible always seem to go when they are in search for God's will for their lives. Moses heads into the desert wilderness of Midian. You see, the most important words of Moses have yet to be spoken! His greatest opportunity for truth-telling, his most significant speaking of truth to power, has yet to come. And before he can do that, before he can speak the words that will eventually liberate the Hebrew people, he heads to Midian where he will spend 40 years! In the wilderness is where he will eventually meet his wife, and where they settle down to raise a family. But, it's also the place where he will hear from God; which is what we see this morning's second Scripture reading.

Hopefully history has taught us all that silence is indeed consent. We've all likely heard the Martin Niemoller quote, that stands boldly in the Holocaust Museum in DC:

"First, they came for the socialists, and I did not speak out – because I was not a socialist. Then they came for the trade unionists, and I did not speak out because I was not a trade unionist. Then they came for the Jews, and I did not speak out because I was not a Jew. Then they came for me – and there was not left to speak for me.

I hope we all know that having the courage to speak up and to speak, in the name of all that is right and good, is always, the right and good thing to do. I hope we all know that. But the story of Moses teaches us something more.

Winston Churchill once said that "courage is what is takes to stand up and speak; but courage is also what it takes to sit down and listen!" And this friends, is a critical lesson from the life of Moses.

What we see in today's second Scripture passage, about Moses before the burning bush, is really representative of what had been happening in Moses life the entire 40 or so years that he was in the desert of Midian: for it was there that he was learning this important lesson – before we speak, we need to listen!

It is interesting to me that the Hebrew word for desert is the word midbaar – and the word that means to speak, is dahbaar. And they're related!

Interesting, isn't it? Perhaps that's why so many Biblical scholars and theologians rightly understand the desert, or the desert experiences of our lives, as being those places . . . where God speaks!

Moses' 40 years in the desert were no doubt hard: they were lonely and parched places, where he struggled, and had to have wondered where God was and what God was preparing him for. But eventually he marries and has a family. And so sometimes his desert experience became rather routine, and mundane. But those 40 years culminate in front of a burning bush where he finally hears God's call upon his life, and at last, he is ready. He has learned about God – about holiness, and reverence, about trust, and obedience. And friends, only then, only after all of that, was Moses ready to go and speak some of the most important words of his life . . . "Let my people go!"

Church, the greatest words of Moses were spoken to the man who raised him, Egypt's Pharaoh. But before they could be spoken, Moses needed to be listening to God, in the desert of Midian, and in the burning bush. In both places, perhaps in all places, we stand on holy ground, which is perhaps what the mindful life, or the contemplative life, are really all about: standing on holy ground, and listening.

Looking back on my life I can't tell you how many times my prayers have been about little more than crying out to God to speak to me! "What should I do God?" "How should I respond?" "Where should I go?" "God, speak, would you! Please! Speak!"

But I've slowly come to discover that asking God to speak, is like asking the oceans to stay wet! God is always speaking. The Spirit is always moving. We're just not listening. We just not paying attention! Which is why more and more I'm beginning to believe that the faithful life is just becoming more intentional mindful of the Spirit's movement in our lives, each and every day, so that we can better listen to all that the Spirit is saying to us.

The world is full of people today who believe that God is calling them to speak . . . to speak out against evil and injustice, to condemn infanticide and defend the rights of the marginalized, to address all the 'isms' that continue to tear our country apart. We all think we've been give the gift of prophecy, and that like Moses, the Spirit is not just calling us, but rather demanding us, to speak up, and to realize that silence is indeed consent. And frankly, that's exciting to me.

But before any of us speak, let's make sure we're listening! Let's be sure that we are reading, and studying Scripture, so that we might glean some of the wisdom that has been shaping and molding the life of the faith community for generations. Let's be sure we're gathering with other people of faith, in setting like this . . . yes . . . with like-minded people focusing on the same Christ and learning the ways of the one who 2000 years ago changed the course of human history. And let's also be sure we're recognizing God's work and movement isn't confined to this place, and with people just like us . . . but rather develop eyes that can see the Spirit at all times and in all people and places. And let's be sure that even in the parched and painful, even in the mediocre and mundane, we're listening for the Spirit of the Christ to speak into our lives, empowering and equipping us to become part of all that God is doing in the world.

Folks, we've all got an awful lot to say. But before we say any more, let's learn to listen, to one another, but especially to God! Like Moses, let's watch for the burning bushes of our lives, and reverently stand quietly, shoeless, and awed. And in those holy moments, on holy ground, let's listen!

Let's just be still and listen!

Passion Parables:
The Resistance of the Palms
April 14, 2019

Luke 19:28-40

After he had said this, he went on ahead, going up to Jerusalem.

When he had come near Bethphage and Bethany, at the place called the Mount of Olives, he sent two of the disciples, saying, "Go into the village ahead of you, and as you enter it you will find tied there a colt that has never been ridden. Untie it and bring it here. If anyone asks you, 'Why are you untying it?' just say this, 'The Lord needs it.'"

So those who were sent departed and found it as he had told them. As they were untying the colt, its owners asked them, "Why are you untying the colt?" They said, "The Lord needs it."

Then they brought it to Jesus; and after throwing their cloaks on the colt, they set Jesus on it. As he rode along, people kept spreading their cloaks on the road. As he was now approaching the path down from the Mount of Olives, the whole multitude of the disciples began to praise God joyfully with a loud voice for all the deeds of power that they had seen, saying, "Blessed is the king who comes in the name of the Lord! Peace in heaven, and glory in the highest heaven!"

Some of the Pharisees in the crowd said to him, "Teacher, order your disciples to stop." He answered, "I tell you, if these were silent, the stones would shout out."

Luke 15:1-10

Now all the tax collectors and sinners were coming near to listen to him. And the Pharisees and the scribes were grumbling and saying, "This fellow welcomes sinners and eats with them."

So he told them this parable: "Which one of you, having a hundred sheep and losing one of them, does not leave the ninety-nine in the wilderness and go after the one that is lost until he finds it? When he has found it, he lays it on his shoulders and rejoices. And when he comes home, he calls together his friends and neighbors, saying to them, 'Rejoice with me, for I have found my sheep that was lost.' Just so, I tell you, there will be more joy in heaven over one sinner who repents than over ninety-nine righteous persons who need no repentance.

"Or what woman having ten silver coins, if she loses one of them, does not light a lamp, sweep the house, and search carefully until she finds it? When she has found it, she calls together her friends and neighbors, saying, 'Rejoice with me, for I have found the coin that I had lost.'

Just so, I tell you, there is joy in the presence of the angels of God over one sinner who repents."

Last week I spoke about hell, or the word used in Greek – Gehenna. And while we all may have a slightly different take on what we think hell is like, for my wife, the best comparison is without a doubt – the Potomac Mills Outlet Mall! Jeanne hates shopping, and so spending any amount of time in a place like Potomac Mills, for her, really is nothing short of . . . hell!

But the same cannot be said for my sister-in-law! Jeanne's brother Kim, his wife Dorte, and their two oldest sons, then, like 18 and 20, were here for our son Jacob's wedding two years ago; and on the Friday before all of the celebrations, they decided to head down to Potomac Mills to do some shopping. So they got there at 10:00am sharp, right when the place opened, and without even talking to one another about meeting up, they simply scatted and began hitting all of their favorite stores . . . which to this day, I still don't understand . . . because well before lunch, they couldn't find my sister-is-law. Her Danish phone wasn't working here in the States and so there was no way to contact her. Needless to say, when Kim called and told us that he and his sons couldn't find his wife, we imagined the worse! We had visions of her having been kidnapped by MS-13, laying in a ditch somewhere, dead! So it was a crazy 6 hours . . . as anyone who has ever lost a child, or . . . in this case, a parent . . . knows. When a loved one is lost, it's torture, right? Dorte eventually turned up! But I can't even begin imagine what it's like when such a reunion never comes.

Perhaps that's why this morning's parables are so powerful – because they're all about something being lost. Just as Jesus tells a variety of kindom parables, which we considered last week; so too does Luke give an account of Jesus telling several parables dealing with the lost: three to be exact. And this morning we're going to look at the first two.

Now each is a wonderful story lifting up God's concern for that which is indeed lost. Whether a sheep or a coin, God cares! Neither appears to have all that much value, at least not in the eyes of the world; but as far God is concerned – as far as the shepherd is concerned or the woman is concerned – nothing is more important than that that one lost sheep or that one lost coin. Even though leaving 99 sheep to find 1 that has wandered away, doesn't exactly appear to be the sharpest shepherding move, that is precisely what happens. Because that one lost sheep is so important to the shepherd!

And that silver coin, that the woman was trying to find? It was one little coin, maybe worth a day's wages: not really all that much . . . unless one is living in poverty.   Because then it could be life-sustaining! Which is why in both instances, when the shepherd and the woman, upon finding that for which they were so desperately searching, they invite their friends and neighbors over to celebrate. Their passionate care and concern for that which they had lost was clear; and so they were willing to do whatever needed to be done, and to give up whatever needed to be given up, in order to find the sheep and the coin.

Now as we've seen over the past few weeks, many of the parables that Jesus tells, involve God; and that is certainly true this morning. So who represents God in each of these two stories?

Exactly! In the first one, the shepherd represents God; and in the second one it's the woman who represents God. (Interestingly, Luke is the most inclusive of all four accounts of the Gospel, and so he is always lifting up women. It shouldn't surprise us at all, that he remembers Jesus portraying God as a woman!)

But in both instances, what he is trying to show us is that God is always committed to finding those who are lost. On display for us, in these two short parables, is the Divine commitment to those who appear to have little value and who are not where they should be. And we see God's choice to do whatever needs to be done to go after them. Because those who are lost are very simply, not in the possession of the one who loves them, and values them, and seeks to care for them. The lost are not in the arms of the one to whom they belong! And Jesus' mission is always to correct that!

We have to remember why Jesus was telling these parables in the first place. He was talking to the tax collectors and sinners, right? And the Scribes and Pharisees were ticked. Jesus knows they're listening in to what he is saying, and so we're given the impression that he tells this story as much for them, as for the tax collectors and sinners. He apparently wants everyone to know that he has come for the lost! He wants the tax collectors and the sinners to know that, but he also wants the elite, religious folk, who think that he came just for them, to know that his greater concern is for those who are lost.

I know I say this all the time but while Jesus has certainly come for all of us, his particular concern is for those on the margins. He is always drawn to those on the fringe, to those that society is quick to look down upon the sick and ostracized, the poor and the powerless, the lost and alone. And friends, it wasn't just the religious, the Scribes and the Pharisees, who were cutting these people out of the kindom. Rome was doing the very same thing. The government was all about the haves, with little regard for the have-nots. It was all about the rich getting richer and the poor getting poorer; the powerful getting more and the powerless getting less! And Jesus saw that, and knew that, and was all about confronting it. His ministry challenged such a structure, and his ministry was about making it clear that such systemic injustice is simply not a part of God's reign in the world. It has no place in the kindom that he came to inaugurate!

And this is what the Palm Sunday story is all about. Palm Sunday is about Jesus challenging, not so much the religious establishment, but Rome! The empire's negligent attitude towards the lost greatly disturbed Jesus; even more than the attitudes of the scribes and the Pharisees disturbed him. The actions of the empire stood in direct opposition to the things of God, and so Jesus had a choice to make to either side with that empire, or to side with the lost. And his choice, was always for the lost.

And again Church, this is what Palm Sunday is all about. It's about Jesus' choosing to side with the lost, evident in all the events that we seek to remember this day.

Now I don't know about you, but it wasn't until well into my ministry that I realized the incredible significance of what Jesus was actually doing that day. Perhaps like you, when I was growing up, Palm Sunday was a day when we remembered a first century parade in which Jesus hopped on a donkey, because parades didn't have floats back then; and then rode into town, where people were cheering, and celebrating his arrival, the way one might celebrate any esteemed member of a community. They grabbed palm branches, and laid their cloaks on the ground, and they boldly and joyfully celebrated the promised Messiah who had finally come to be among them.

That's what I thought Palm Sunday was all about a parade for Jesus! That was the extent of my theological understanding of this event marking the beginning of Holy Week. And so what better way for the church to celebrate that, than by giving the little kids palm branches to wave, while we adults sing our hosanna songs and hymns? What better way to remember these events than with kids waving palm branches and adults singing hosanna! That's Palm Sunday, right?

Well! No! That is NOT why we're here this morning. Because that is NOT what Palm Sunday is all about. That would be like thinking that "West Side Story" is about dancers in New York City in the 1950s. That would be like thinking that the story of "Roots" is about African immigration to America . . . or that "Three Billboards Outside of Ebbing, Missouri" is about advertising in the Midwest!

Palm Sunday is not about: a parade for Jesus. And so this morning the kids aren't going to process with palm branches. The choir isn't going to parade down the center aisle singing hosanna to the King of Kings. We haven't planned any of that this year because that is not what Palm Sunday is all about. Rather, Palm Sunday is about a choice. It's about Jesus' choice, to stand with the lost. It's about his standing up to and against Rome, because the politics of Rome was seeking to stand over and again the politics of God.

I've grown quite weary of hearing people saying that politics has no place in the Church. Because friends the Gospel of Jesus Christ is about nothing if is not about the politics of the day. And nothing makes that more apparent than the events of Palm Sunday.

So for those of you, who for one reason or another, will miss all the events of Holy Week, and therefore simply move from the praises of Palm Sunday to the praises of Easter Sunday, and forget everything that happened in between: well then, this morning's worship is for you! Because what I want to do this morning is set the stage for Easter, so that we might all have a better understanding of what the crucifixion was all about. I want to try and help us all better understand why Jesus was put on the cross in the first place. And it was all about this choice! It's about a choice he made his entire life: but that he very intentionally thrust into the face of Rome on Palm Sunday. And that choice was, and remains, always, for the lost.

You see Jesus wasn't the only one who went to Jerusalem for Passover that week. Pilate went as well, as the harbinger of Rome, to keep the peace in what would become a very crowded city. But unlike Jesus, when Pilate rode into Jerusalem, he didn't arrive on a donkey. Pilate rode into town on a horse, surrounded by chariots and foot soldiers. And unlike Jesus, he didn't enter from the east, he came from the west, the gate through which the powerful always entered Jerusalem.

This is why the Palm Sunday story is so remarkably political. Because as a way of challenging Rome, and standing against the powerful, Jesus choice to side with the lost. He gave us a glimpse into the heart of God by opposing any worldview that might confuse The Roman Empire with the Kindom of God. This is what is at the heart of the Palm Sunday proclamation. Jesus is our king, not Caesar; and as the God-man here on earth, his concern is for the lost . . . and not just lost sheep, or coins, but people. People on the margins. People overlooked and undervalued. People ignored and neglected. People left out and people pushed aside.

Palm Sunday is about Jesus making the conscience choice to stand against the evil of empire. He wasn't crucified because he offended the religious establishment. If his death had anything to do with the Jewish religion, he would have been stoned. But he wasn't stoned, he was crucified . . . he suffered the punishment of Roman traitors because he directly challenged Rome . . . because his choices stood in direct opposition to any theology of empire.

I can't presume to know what was in the hearts of Jesus followers 2000 years ago, nor presume to know how much they really understood about what was happening. But what I DO know, and what I CAN claim today, is that taking a palm branch, as a sign of our allegiance to Jesus, is an act of naming Him as our king. It's an act of claiming God's ways, to be our ways. It's an act of choosing to side with the Spirit and to stand on the side of the lost.

So for us today, palms are just as much a symbol of resistance, as they are a symbol of praise. They are a sign that we, like Jesus, are willing to speak truth to power, and as someone so brilliantly said to me after worship last week: "to do whatever we can to encourage power to listen to truth."

Palms are a sign that we too, like Jesus, are willing to challenge the thinking of empire: of conquest and colonization, of power and self-preservation, of accumulation and acquisition. They are a sign that we, like Jesus, are committed to being an ally to those whose lives are continually devalued, and whose worth is constantly called into question.

So friends, during this morning's offering, I am going to invite you forward to take a palm from the chancel; and I encourage you to do so mindfully, knowing that what you will be taking home with you is a sign of resistance; a mark that you are willing to be numbered with those standing on the side of the lost, and that YOU, are willing to be identified as a follower of the Anointed One . . . the King of Kings, and Lords of Lords . . . a follower of the One who stands against the powers and principalities of this world . . . a follower of a rebel, the revolutionary the leader of that first century resistance movement . . . Jesus, the Christ.

As our ushers receive this morning's offering, come, if you dare. Take palm, and acknowledge Jesus, as your Lord of Lords, your kind of kings. For blessed is he who comes in the name of the Lord, hosanna in the highest!

The Last Word – "Castrated Converts"
April 29, 2018

As difficult as the presidency of Donald Trump has been for so many Americans, people of faith can never lose hope. As these sermons have sought to remind us, we are citizens of another 'kin'dom. We have grander lord, a bigger god, and a greater love! And just as our faith is about nothing if it is not about our politics; following Jesus is about nothing if it is not about love.

Living in the tension of speaking with a prophetic voice, while at the same time striving to love everyone, is always difficult. But that is the call of the Gospel. And so I offer one more sermon as the 'last word' on the current state of our nation. For as I have stated again and again, the Church MUST speak truth to power. Silence IS consent. And when it comes to justice, kindness, and compassion, there is really no room for debate.

BUT, as we work for the kindom and pursue the things of God, we can never lose the love of Jesus. For indeed, "God is love . . . and if we do not love, we do not know God."

This remains MY greatest challenge. And I hope it is yours as well. This last sermon calls us to this end . . . as does one of the songs we used in worship the Sunday it was preached. The lyrics, by Shawn Gallaway, spoke as powerfully as any Scripture passage or sermon ever could.

I can see laughter, or I can see tears
I see a choice of love or fear
What do you choose?
I can see peace, or I can see war
I can see sunshine, or I can see a storm
What do you choose?
I choose to love with freedom fire
From my heart where the light keeps shining
And I choose to feel the whole world crying
for the strength that we can rise above

I choose love, I choose love

I can see sharing or I can see greed
I can see caring or poverty
What do you choose?
I can see gardens, or I can see flaws
I can see life or death coming on strong
So what do you choose?
I choose to love with freedom fire
From my heart where the light keeps shining
And I choose to feel the whole world crying
for the strength that we can rise above

I choose love, I choose love

I see us healing, darkness dying
I see us dawning as one world united
So what do you choose?
Love or fear?
Oh, what do you choose?
I choose to love with freedom fire
From my heart where the light keeps shining
And I choose to feel the whole world crying
And I choose to feel the one voice rising
And I choose to feel us all united in the strength that we can rise above

I choose love, I choose love, I choose love

Psalm 22:25-31

I offer praise in the great congregation because of you; I will fulfill my promises in the presence of those who honor God. Let all those who are suffering eat and be full! Let all who seek the Lord praise him! I pray your hearts live forever! Every part of the earth will remember and come back to the Lord; every family among all the nations will worship you. Because the right to rule belongs to the Lord, he rules all nations. Indeed, all the earth's powerful will worship him; all who are descending to the dust will kneel before him; my being also lives for him. Future descendants will serve him; generations to come will be told about my Lord. They will proclaim God's righteousness to those not yet born, telling them what God has done.

Acts 8:26-40

An angel from the Lord spoke to Philip, "At noon, take[a] the road that leads from Jerusalem to Gaza." So he did. Meanwhile, an Ethiopian man was on his way home from Jerusalem, where he had come to worship. He was a eunuch and an official responsible for the entire treasury of Candace (. . . the . . . Ethiopian queen.) He was reading the prophet Isaiah while sitting in his carriage. The Spirit told Philip, "Approach this carriage and stay with it." Running up to the carriage, Philip heard the man reading the prophet Isaiah. He asked, "Do you really understand what you are reading?" The man replied, "Without someone to guide me, how could I?" Then he invited Philip to climb up and sit with him. This was the passage of scripture he was reading: Like a sheep he was led to the slaughter and like a lamb before its shearer is silent, so he didn't open his mouth. In his humiliation justice was taken away from him. Who can tell the story of his descendants because his life was taken from the earth? The eunuch asked Philip, "Tell me, about whom does the prophet say this? Is he talking about himself or someone else?" Starting with that passage, Philip proclaimed the good news about Jesus to him. As they went down the road, they came to some water. The eunuch said, "Look! Water! What would keep me from being baptized?" He ordered that the carriage halt. Both Philip and the eunuch went down to the water, where Philip baptized him. When they came up out of the water, the Lord's Spirit suddenly took Philip away. The eunuch never saw him again but went on his way rejoicing. Philip found himself in Azotus. He traveled through that area, preaching the good news in all the cities until he reached Caesarea.

I'm not sure there's a busier road around – 95 south, Memorial Day weekend! It was definitely NOT the place I wanted to be the last weekend in May. I was dreading the trip but had been asked to speak at a small church gathering just south of Richmond, and I couldn't say 'no'! In spite of the fact I knew traffic would be horrendous, my gut told me that I really needed to be there.

You don't know that about me, but that's often how the Spirit speaks into my life, through my gut.

Actually, you don't know me at all.

I'm Phil, named after the dude in Acts 8: not the apostle Philip, one of Jesus' 12 friends. He was a different guy. I was named after the one appointed by the apostles in the first century, to be a deacon, and to help care for all the people who were becoming part of the growing church. He is my namesake; and like him, that's what I do today. I travel around the state: preaching, teaching, and encouraging people in their walks with God. And generally I love it . . . until, it puts me on 95 south, on a holiday weekend.

As always, it was bumper to bumper all the way through Stafford. But I had expected that. So my sunroof was open, I had my yoga station on Pandora cranked up to keep me calm and was just trying to chill and enjoy what was looking like a beautiful day. But the further south I got, the worse the traffic became. And so when things didn't lighten up after Fredericksburg, where it usually does, I decided to just pull over and take a break.

Like your pastor, my 'pit-stop' of choice is usually Starbucks. But I was in Ladysmith, Virginia, and like most rural areas in the Old Dominion, the closest thing to a Starbucks was MacDonald's. So, since their ice cream cones are only a buck, and they have free wifi, that's where I wound up.

Now I have to be honest, I wasn't excited about where I was. I'll freely admit it. When I leave the DC bubble, as some like to refer to it, and head south, I usually become very sad at what I see. Because some of those small towns along the 95 corridor. . . . well, sometimes they kinda' scare me.

You know what I mean, right?

C'mon, don't pretend you're all that different from me . . . pickups, with the seductively-sitting-silver-women mud flaps . . . 'Don't tread on me license plates' . . . bumper stickers that say things like "Keep honking: I'm reloading."

I know I'm generalizing, but the Confederate flag still flies pretty high in some of those areas, enough to sometimes make you wonder if the south really is getting ready to rise again.

Never-the-less, on this particular weekend, these were the people to whom God was calling me. And I knew that. I knew that because these people were the people that were so hard for me to love. And more often than not, those are the ones to whom we're ALL called.

So I pulled into MickyDs, settled into a booth by the side windows, away from all the commotion of the front counters, and opened my laptop. As I was finishing up my ice cream cone, this clean cut, well-dressed guy in cowboy boots, comes and sits down at one of the tables next to me. He's got a large order of fries, a big bottle of water . . . AND . . . you guessed it . . . a Bible: what looks like a brand new, shiny leather-covered Bible! He pulls out his earbuds, and I can hear Dirks Bentley singing about a beach, somewhere; and he quickly turns off the music. As he begins to enjoy his fries, he glances around, notices me, and gives me a nod.

But before I can nod back, he looks away, opens his Bible, and carefully begins turning the pages, clearly looking for a specific passage. He continues to munch on his fries, two or three at a time, wiping the salt from his fingers after each mouthful.

Now . . . yeah, I'm definitely a pastor-type . . . a Christ-follower, who loves Jesus . . . but that doesn't mean that I want to have a Bible study with every person I meet. I know what you're probably thinking. But really, I'm not one of those guys who gets on a plane and tries convert the poor soul, lucky enough to be sitting next to me. That's not me . . . AT ALL.

BUT . . . THIS . . . this was just too coincidental NOT to be a God-thing. I mean, I don't have a lot of instances where people sit down beside me and open up a Bible. So how could I pass this up?

"Why are the pages of Bibles always so thin?" I asked.

Without looking at me he said, "The other day I actually tore out the last chapter of Jonah trying to get the New Testament," he said, smiling. "When I die, and my kids read this thing and they're going to think that Jonah never got out of the belly of that whale."

'Newby,' I thought. 'It was a 'big fish', not a whale.'

"You from around here?" I asked.

"New Kent," he said, "but the traffic is crazy out there. So I thought I'd stop for a while and maybe it'll thin out."

He wiped his mouth, and I noticed a black swastika tattoo on the inside of his right wrist.

'Naturally,' I thought, and quickly looked up at his face, before he could catch me staring at it. "So . . . what are ya' readin'?" I said.

"I just started Acts."

"You part of a church?" I went on.

"No, but I have a nephew at Liberty University, who just . . . 'got saved,' and so he's been on my case about reading the Bible. He told me to start with John. So when I finished it a couple days ago, I just kept going."

"Liberty?" I said, "Interesting place!"

"Yeah, it really is. And the more he tells me about it, the more I like what it stands for. He's not a big fan of Falwell's politics, but I don't know, I appreciate what he has to say, even though I'm not very religious."

"What do you mean?" I asked, not really sure I wanted to hear his answer.

"Well I like the idea of 'making American great again.' I'm not really into all that LGTQ stuff . . . and Black Lives Matter . . . and Me Too! I guess I just don't understand why so many people have gotten so down on America, and the south, and the cops, and the National Anthem, and everything else."

Realizing very quickly that I should probably change the subject, I decided to get back to the Bible. "So tell me, where are you in Acts?"

"Well, some guy named Stephen was just stoned to death."

"Ah, ok, so you've not gotten to Philip and the Ethiopian eunuch yet?" I said. "Philip is my namesake."

"Cool," he said. "So that's your name, Phil."

"Yup!"

"Hey, I'm Lyle, nice to meet you."

"Yeah, nice to meet you too," I said.

"So . . ." he paused, "what exactly is a eunuch."

As I began pulling up my Bible on my computer, I decided to get straight to the heart of the story. "Well, let's just say they were outcasts, in all kinds of ways. eunuchs were . . . different . . . and people back then really didn't like different. They didn't understand it. You see eunuchs . . . couldn't be circumcised . . . if you know what I mean . . . so there was no way they could ever become Jewish, or part of the faith community."

"I don't get it," he said.

"Well, in the very early days of the church, it was believed that to follow Jesus, first people needed to become Jewish. And since eunuchs couldn't be circumcised, they couldn't. So they were just looked down upon. They were people on the margins of society . . . everywhere . . . outcasts in every sense of the word. But Philip . . . Philip told him that God still loved him and cared for him."

"Cool," Lyle said, looking surprisingly interested in all that I was saying.

"They met on a road not quite as busy as 95," I continued, "but almost. And so their paths crossed, and they wound up getting into this great conversation about the Bible. And Philip took advantage of the opportunity to just assure the guy that God doesn't just love CERTAIN people, but God's love is for everyone . . . no exceptions."

"You a preacher?" Lyle said, after a short pause.

"How'd you guess?" I asked. "You sat down at just the right table! Lucky you!"

"Cool," he said again, smiling. "So . . . God loves everyone? . . . even," he hesitated, "Hitler?"

"God always chooses love over hate. And I think that's how we're supposed to love too; unconditionally! We're supposed to love everyone . . . LGBTQ people, Nazis . . . everyone . . . especially those we don't WANT to love!"

He was now staring out the window; and then slowly, pensively, almost sadly, I saw him roll over his wrist, look down at it, and then turn his eyes towards me.

"Everyone," I said, "God loves everyone!"

Neither of us said anything for a few moments, and then Lyle said, "So whatever happened to the Eunuch?"

"Well, I guess he got the message, because he asked Philip to baptize him, and Philip did, and then they both went on their way. Guess you could say he became a castrated convert!"

"Hmmm," he said.

Silence settled over us once again, and it was pretty clear Lyle was done talking. "Guess WE should probably be on OUR way," he said.

I nodded, and smiled, and then got up.

"I was great meeting you Lyle," I said. "Thanks for the good conversation." And with that, I reached over the table to try and shake his hand, and accidently knocked his water bottle all over his leather Bible. Before either of us could pick it up, water – what looked like gallons of it – was rolling off the table, into his lap, and down his pant leg.

"I'm so sorry," I said, as he stood up laughing.

"No biggie," he said, trying to wipe off his Bible with the one napkin left on his tray.

I ran to get some more, and when I came back, he was still laughing. "You know," I've already been baptized!"

"Really," I said, chuckling.

"Yeah, some little Presbyterian Church, on the Eastern Shore - that's where I grew up."

"Well then you already know everything we just talked about," I said, putting all the wet napkins on his tray. "Baptism is all about God's love for all of us . . . no matter what. It's always there and it never ends."

I looked at him. And he looked at me. "Don't forget that," I said.

His eyes were moist, his smile faint.

"I'm going to be driving for another hour in wet pants. Forgetting that is not likely!" he said, bursting out in laughter.

I shook his hand, and then walked out to my car. I threw my computer bag in the back seat and saw that the traffic on 95 had indeed died down. I left the parking lot, accelerated down the long entrance ramp on 95 South, and made my way out to the passing lanes where traffic was moving at a nice clip.

'Nice guy,' I thought to myself. 'Glad I took the time to notice.'

After a few minutes, I felt a raindrop hit my cheek, and noticed that the sunny skies had given way to clouds. I went to close the sunroof, but then stopped. Another drop hit my shoulder, and I smiled to myself. I couldn't get my own words out of my head.

"Everyone! God loves everyone! No matter what. Don't forget that."

Rural rednecks. Crazy Christians. Confederate, flag-flying Nazis. God loves all of us. All the people that we want to push to the margins of our lives . . . are loved by God . . . dearly, and deeply. No matter how crazy their beliefs. No matter how evil their behavior. No matter how absurdly distorted their worldview . . . they are children of God. And the baptismal waters that have claimed them, are the very same waters that have claimed me.

'Sometimes God makes me laugh,' I thought. I had just encountered Jesus, at a MacDonald's off of 95 South, in Ladysmith, VA, in a guy with a swastika tattoo. I was reminded that at the foot of the cross, we're all the same height. And God loves us every one of us!

A smile wouldn't leave my face. And water began soaking my head, and my shirt. But I didn't care.

I just kept driving.

And it just kept raining.